M42 Duster

A VISUAL HISTORY OF THE U.S. ARMY'S MODERN MOBILE ANTIAIRCRAFT PLATFORM

by David Doyle

Published by
Ampersand Group, Inc.
A HobbyLink Japan company
235 NE 6th Ave., Suite B
Delray Beach, FL 33483-5543
561-266-9686 • 561-26609786 Fax
www.ampersandpubco.com • www.hlj.com

Acknowledgements:
This book would have been impossible to create without the generous assistance of many individuals and institutions, including Paul Kopsick, historian of the National Dusters, Quads, and Searchlights Association, Allan Cors and Marc Sehring of the National Museum of Americans in Wartime, the Air Defense Artillery Museum, Tom Kailbourn, Scott Taylor, John Adams-Graf, Stuart Robinson and the late Richard Hunnicutt. Special thanks to my wife Denise, who not only provided moral support—but also scanned the bulk of the vintage images in this book.

Sources:
Sheridan, A history of the American Light Tank, Volume 2, by R.P. Hunnicutt, Presidio Press, Novato, California, 1995

TM9-761A, Self-propelled Twin 40mm Gun T141, Department of the Army, Washington, DC, 8 May 1952.

TM9-7218 Twin 40mm Full Tracked Self-propelled Gun M42 (T141), Department of the Army, Washington, DC, 21 May 1957.

TM 9-2350-202-ESC Equipment Serviceability Criteria for Gun, Antiaircraft Artillery, Self-Propelled: Twin 40-mm, M42 and M42A1, Washington, DC, 21 May 1969.

TM 9-2350-202-20P, Technical Manual, Organizational Maintenance Repair Parts and Special Tools Lists, Gun, Self-Propelled: Twin, 40-MM, M42 and M42A1 (2350-049-4791), 14 September 1972.

OCM Item 33869, 9 May 1952.

OCM Item 35012, 22 October 1953.

OCM item 35297, 6 May 1954.

OCM item 36084, 2 February 1956.

OCM item 36084, 2 February 1956.

Aberdeen Proving Ground Third Memorandum Report, 16 June 1955.

Cover: This example of an M42A1 registration number 40228548, served with the 4th Battalion, 60th Artillery, and was performing a defensive role at a fire-support base in Dak To Province during Operation Greely in July 1967. Also see page 29. (NARA)

Title page: Two M42A1 twin 40mm Automatic Weapons Self-Propelled, (AW SP) of 140 Section of Charlie Battery 4th BN, 60th ADA roll into LZ Two Bits, (Binh Dinh Prov.) 9 August 1967. All hands seem to be wary, including the track commander (or squad leader) of the lead vehicle, who is standing up in his hatch holding an M16 rifle and wearing a flak vest and combat vehicle crewman's (CVC) helmet. (NARA)

Introduction, top: Photographed at U.S. Army Base F, Finschhafen, New Guinea on November 9, 1944, this vehicle was called the M15 Special. It was a M15 multiple-gun motor carriage with an M1 40mm cannon installed in place of the M15's usual use of one 37mm Gun M1 and two M2 Browning .50 caliber machine guns. In particular, the M15 Special saw use in the U.S. invasion of the Philippines. (Patton Museum)

Introduction, bottom: This M19 is of the 3rd AAA and is attached to the 3rd Infantry Division. The guns are pointed up in air defensive posture although no clips of ammo are observed. The gunner has an M24C reflex site in place of speed ring site, and the vehicle has a 1-ton Ben Hur-type trailer in tow. (Air Defense Artillery Museum)

Introduction

Tactical air power truly came into its own during World War II. Formations of men and equipment on the ground were proven to be highly vulnerable to nimble, bomb-laden strafing aircraft. Engineers and strategists on all sides struggled to develop mobile antiaircraft weaponry to combat this threat. One of the most powerful, reliable and feared weapons was the Bofors 40mm automatic cannon. Developed by the Swedish firm AB Bofors, this weapon was used by both the Allies and the Axis during WWII, a testament to its sound design.

The U.S. Navy used many different mountings for the Bofors during WWII, most notably the quadruple mounts that covered battleships, cruisers and aircraft carriers. The U.S. Army used the Bofors during WWII as well, typically on a towed single-barrel mounting called the "40mm Automatic Gun M1." Late in the war the twin-cannon M19 Gun Motor Carriage, a self-propelled vehicle, was developed but this did not see field use during WWII.

With the outbreak of the Korean War the M19 saw considerable service as part of several antiaircraft artillery (AAA) units, seeing

most of their action in ground supporting roles against enemy personnel and emplacements.

However, by that time the U.S. Army had begun efforts to modernize its tactical vehicle fleet, as well as standardize components. In 1951, the Army began developing an upgrade to the M19 system. The result was the M42, a member of the M41 family of armored vehicles, all of which shared several common mechanical components.

The Cadillac Motor Car Division of General Motors delivered the lead vehicle of the type, given the trial designation of T141, in August 1951. The rear of the hull and its power train, including the Continental AOS-895-3 air-cooled engine and Allison CD-500-3 cross drive transmission, as well as the suspension, were common to both the T41, precursor to the M41, and the T141, precursor to the M42.

Once accepted by the military, procurement was begun immediately, with American Car and Foundry (ACF Industries) joining Cadillac in producing the vehicles in April 1952. Despite entering production by both manufacturers in 1952, the vehicle, by then known as the "Duster," was not type classified as Standard and designated M42 until October 1953.

Like the WWII-designed M19, the M42 was armed with dual automatic Bofors M2A1 40mm antiaircraft cannon. At the muzzle of the guns of the early production vehicles were conical flash suppressors, resembling those used on the 40mm weapons in naval service. These would give way on later production vehicles to three-prong style flash suppressors, of which two types were produced.

Early production vehicles could also be distinguished by the two doors between the driver's and commander's hatches on the upper surface of the hulls. When opened, the intent was that ammunition cans could be passed from the hull to the mount. Evidently this feature was of little utility as these doors were eliminated on later vehicles. Attached to the side armor of the rotating 40mm mount was a machine gun pintle. Originally, a .30-caliber GPMG replaced the M1919. This was but one of the upgrades that the Duster received during its service life. Other improvements included updated communications equipment and the replacement of the carbureted engine with a fuel injected version yielding improved performance and range. Vehicles so upgraded were classified M42A1.

The M42 was deployed stateside and in many international locations, but was considered by many to be outdated and unable to support ground troops in the new age of jet aircraft and later on, jet helicopters. Most M42s were relegated to National Guard units in Delaware, Florida, New Mexico, Michigan, Ohio and other states.

However, as U.S. involvement in Vietnam escalated, three Duster Battalions that were deployed between 1966 and 1971. The 1st Bn 44th ADA was the first to arrive and was deployed in the north and was attached to the 3rd Marine Regiment (ICORP, IFFV). The 5th Bn 2nd ADA was the second to arrive and was deployed in the south (III CORP, IIFFV). The 4th Bn 60th ADA arrived last and deployed in the Central Highlands (IICORP, IFFV) The Dusters were typically deployed in pairs, with four Dusters comprising a section. Two sections (1st and 2nd) comprised a platoon of eight and two platoons (1st and 2nd) comprised the battery of 16 Dusters. There were four batteries (A, B, C, and D), plus spare vehicles held under the commanding Headquarters battery.

The next phase in the U.S. fully tracked and armored antiaircraft system was the T141 project. Based on the chassis of the M41 Walker light tank, it moved the twin-40mm mount farther forward on the hull. Originally, the fire of the T141's guns was to be directed remotely by a radar fire-control system. (Patton Museum) **Inset:** This 10 May 1951 photo of the T141 mockup indicates that there originally were or were intended to be three hinged doors below the stowage box on the left side of the vehicle and only one spare barrel. This feature was not present on the production M42 as two spare barrels were placed there. Knapsacks are secured to the gun mount and front of the stowage box, and two .30-caliber machine guns are on pintle mounts on the 40mm gun mount. The barrel of a second .30-caliber machine gun is visible above the gunner's position. Side mud guards are attached which require the flat style front and rear fenders. Later models have tapered front and rear fenders, as the side mud panels were abandoned. (TACOM LCMC History Office)

An M42 is under construction to the right on the final-assembly line at the Cadillac Motor Car Division of the Cleveland Tank Plant. This vehicle was sharing the assembly line with a number of M41 light tanks. The 40mm guns, complete with flash suppressors, have been mounted. (Patton Museum)

T141 U.S. Army registration number 40228157 is part of what appears to be a factory instructional or analytical display that also includes an M41 tank and several M41 turrets on stands. In the left background is a T141 mount on a stand. (Patton Museum)

A T141 poses next to an M41 light tank. Delivery of the T141 to the U.S. Army began in August 1951. The simple tri-forked flash suppressor replaced the older conical version that was used on early examples of the T141 and the standardized M42. (National Dusters, Quads and Searchlights Association)

Top left: Stenciled on the hull door of this vehicle is "T141 TWIN 40MM." The tracks on these vehicles were the T91E3, of steel construction with replaceable rubber pads on the outside. There were 75 shoes per track assembly. **Top right:** Viewed from the left side, the forward positioning of the T141's gun mount is evident. Oil-bath air cleaners were externally mounted in front of the mufflers, which were located on the top rear of both fenders. At the rear of the 40mm gun mount M4E1 was a pintle for an M1919A4 machine gun. The T141 (RN: 40228156) was standardized as the M42 twin 40mm self-propelled gun on October 22, 1953. **Above left:** A newly minted M42, registration number 12H421, exhibits fresh paint and bright metal on its mufflers below the raised stowage racks over the rear of each fender.

The bare metal muffler for the auxiliary power unit (APU) on the pioneer tool rack on the right rear fender is similarly pristine. With use, these mufflers would soon become rusted and discolored from exhaust heat and exposure to the elements. (Patton Museum, three) **Above right:** Two children marvel at an M42 on display in the Dallas, Texas area around 1960. The front hinges for the overhead doors between the driver's and commander's hatches are visible at the top of the glacis. On the front door is a box for .30-caliber ammunition and storage clips for a carbine. Later, this box was moved to the left side of the door and mounted vertically, and a storage box for an M19 periscope was mounted at the center of the door. (Air Defense Artillery Museum)

The gun mount of this M42 is traversed to the rear and the muzzles of the 40mm guns are fitted with the conical flash suppressors used early in the production of the M42s. The gun mount could traverse 360 degrees in nine seconds, and the guns had a maximum elevation of 87 degrees under manual control and 85 degrees under powered control. Combined, the two guns could fire 240 rounds per minute. The rack over the muffler on the left rear fender held four spare track links. The two boxes on the rear deck held an M20 3.5" antitank rocket launcher and four rockets. These boxes were discontinued on later-production M42s. (NARA)

General Data

Model	M42	M42A1
Weight*	49500	49500
Max Towed Load	5000	5000
Length**	250.25	250.25
Width**	126 15/16	126 15/16
Height**	112.125	112.125
Track	102.5	102.5
Track Width	21	21
Max Speed	45	45
Fuel Capacity	80	80
Range	100	100
Electrical	24 negative	24 negative
Transmission Speeds	2	2
Turning Radius	Pivot	Pivot

*Fighting weight, all weights listed in pounds.
**Overall dimensions listed in inches. Guns facing forward.

Engine Data

Vehicle Model	M42	M42A1
Engine Make/Model	AOS-895-3	AOSI-895-5
Number of Cylinders	Opposed 6	Opposed 6
Cubic Inch Displacement	895.9	895.9
Horsepower	500 @ 2800	500 @ 2800
Torque	955 @ 2400	955 @ 2400
Governed Speed (Rpm)	2800	2800

Left: This T141 was photographed from overhead during trials at Aberdeen Proving Ground on November 28, 1951. The layout is similar to that of the standardized M42, except that the squared-off front mud guards would be replaced on the M42 by angled ones. Although hard to discern in this view, the T141s and early M42s had two overhead doors on the roof of the driver's and commander's compartment. The joint where these doors met ran between the driver's and commander's hatches. In service, it was found that the doors were rarely used, and they were subsequently discontinued. (US Army Ordnance Museum)

The mount is traversed to the rear on this Twin 40mm Self-propelled Gun M42. Mufflers with tailpipes are near the rear of each fender. To the fronts of the mufflers are the drum-shaped oil-bath air cleaners. A lifting ring was available inboard of each taillight assembly. A mount for a pintle hook is between the two lugs for tow hooks on the lower rear plate of the hull. (Patton Museum)

This M42, registration number 12B871, freshly arrived in Germany. The barrels, recuperators, and flash suppressors of the 40mm guns have been wrapped in paper secured with olive drab tape for shipment. Corrosion has started to set in around the hull and the oil bath air cleaners. Stenciling is present on the equipment and ammunition lockers. On the transmission cover at the upper rear of the hull is the transmission oil filler cover. The louvers on either side of the transmission cover are part of the battery access doors. (Verne Kindschi)

Another view of M42 registration number 12B871 shows the multiple stencils on the ammunition and equipment lockers. In addition to those indicating the locations of the standard equipment such as tow cable, combat packs, and asbestos mittens, there are stencils noting the maintenance history of the vehicle. The gun sight accessory chest is in place to the rear of the gunner's shield. The clean nature of the gun mount indicates that the canvas cover was just removed. (Verne Kindschi)

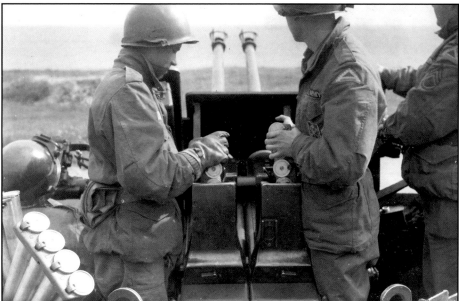

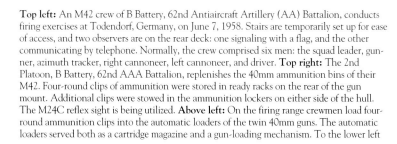

Top left: An M42 crew of B Battery, 62nd Antiaircraft Artillery (AA) Battalion, conducts firing exercises at Todendorf, Germany, on June 7, 1958. Stairs are temporarily set up for ease of access, and two observers are on the rear deck: one signaling with a flag, and the other communicating by telephone. Normally, the crew comprised six men: the squad leader, gunner, azimuth tracker, right cannoneer, left cannoneer, and driver. **Top right:** The 2nd Platoon, B Battery, 62nd AAA Battalion, replenishes the 40mm ammunition bins of their M42. Four-round clips of ammunition were stored in ready racks on the rear of the gun mount. Additional clips were stowed in the ammunition lockers on either side of the hull. The M24C reflex sight is being utilized. **Above left:** On the firing range crewmen load four-round ammunition clips into the automatic loaders of the twin 40mm guns. The automatic loaders served both as a cartridge magazine and a gun-loading mechanism. To the lower left are more clips in a ready rack.

Above right: Private First Class King Reed, the gunner of an M42, was photographed peering through his M24C reflex gun sight on the left side of the gun mount of an M42 of B Battery, 62nd AAA Battalion. As the gunner, he controls both the elevation and traverse of the guns during power-control operation, using the hand grips of the drive controller. He also fires the guns using the triggers on the drive controller hand grips (automatic mode). The gunner could fire a single shot or on full automatic from either left, right or both guns simultaneously. (NARA, all)

Left: While waiting for a target to appear on the firing range at Todendorf, Staff Sergeant Richard Smalley of B Battery, 62nd AAA Battalion, adjusts the automatic lead setter of the M38 computing sight on the right side of the 40mm guns. Smalley was the squad leader of the vehicle, but his many duties included serving as the lead setter when the guns were in powered operation. **Right:** Private First Class Bill Crane of Headquarters Battery, 62nd AAA Battalion, handles a four-round clip of 40mm ammunition in an ammo box with a four-clip capacity. The location was Todendorf, Germany, on 7 June 1958. Stacked in the background are hundreds of individual 40mm round packing tubes. (NARA, both)

Sergeant First Class Melvin Yarborough, a section chief in B Battery, 62nd AAA Battalion, points out a target for his 40mm gun crew to track during a drill at Sullivan Barracks on 28 May 1958. They were practicing for live-firing exercises that were scheduled to begin soon at Todendorf, Germany. A bundle of equipment, including striped aiming stakes, is tied to the ammunition locker. The hold-open latch for the front door is above the left headlight guard. All four visible tracks have angled fenders and the hinges and hold open latches for the overhead hull doors. Several other M42s are visible at the battery's motor park. (NARA)

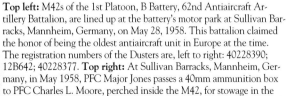

Top left: M42s of the 1st Platoon, B Battery, 62nd Antiaircraft Artillery Battalion, are lined up at the battery's motor park at Sullivan Barracks, Mannheim, Germany, on May 28, 1958. This battalion claimed the honor of being the oldest antiaircraft unit in Europe at the time. The registration numbers of the Dusters are, left to right: 40228390; 12B642; 40228377. **Top right:** At Sullivan Barracks, Mannheim, Germany, in May 1958, PFC Major Jones passes a 40mm ammunition box to PFC Charles L. Moore, perched inside the M42, for stowage in the fighting compartment. In addition to the open door of the commander's hatch at the left, the early-type overhead doors are open, with the front panel appearing over PFC Moore's head and the rear panel leaning against the front of the gun mount. Suspended between the front tow hooks is a sign in English and German that explosives are being handled onboard. **Above left:** The crew of an M42 Duster of A Battery, 2nd Automatic Weapons Battalion (Self-Propelled), 278th Artillery, Alabama National Guard, undergoes firing exercises on the range at Fort Stewart, Georgia. Also onboard are an observer and signalman. The spare barrel rack is empty and conical flash protectors are used. This early example has square front and rear fenders. **Above right:** The crew of an M42 fire at a towed aerial target at "C" Range, Fort Stewart, Georgia, on April 1, 1959. Empty storage boxes for 40mm ammunition are neatly stacked as a stairway to the rear of the vehicle. An observer on the rear deck holds a signal flag. The flash suppressors are the early, conical type as are the square fenders and rear storage boxes. Some smoke is visible in the gun mount probably from spent shell casings being ejected down the deflector chutes. (NARA, all)

Top left: While the cannoneers tend to the 40mm guns, a crewman is at the ready on the .30-caliber machine gun. This M42 with the 50th AAA Gun Battery in South Korea was photographed on October 27, 1956. The wire tow rope secured to the ammunition locker was standard equipment for M42s. Padlocks are attached to several of the T-handles on the equipment lockers below the ammo lockers. The two brackets below the tow rope were for a disassembled cleaning rod, which is not present. **Top right:** Lieutenant Harry J. Klarmen receives firing instructions from the commander of B Battery, 62nd Antiaircraft Artillery Battalion, on the firing range at Todendorf, Germany, 7 June 1958. A wooden beam has been temporarily positioned through the rear lifting eyes to support the stairs provided for the convenience of the observers. Arranged to the front of the soldier to the left are containers for 40mm ammunition. **Above left:** An M42 and crew from 1st Battle Group, 23rd Infantry Regiment were photographed in winter camouflage during Exercise Willow Freeze at Tolsans Lake, Alaska, on 11 February 1961. The gun mount is traversed to the rear, and exhaust vapor is emanating from the muffler at the left. What appear to be clear plastic windscreens are to the front of the driver's and commander's hatches. A small pine tree was placed between the guns, perhaps as camouflage. Winter training exercises such as Willow Freeze would severely test the exposed gun crews. **Above right:** On 29 July 1961, M42 crews of the 1st Battalion, 278th Artillery, conduct summer training exercises at the Pelham Range at Fort McClellan, Alabama. The closest vehicle has a waterproof cover secured over the gun mount, part of which has been rolled back so the gun crew can be at their posts. Dust covers are fitted over the muzzles of the guns. The smoke and dust in the right background is from other 40mm guns being fired. (NARA, all)

Top left: Specialist Fourth Class John Myers sits at his position as gunner of an M42, registration number 12D345, in Alaska on 27 January 1961. His unit, the 1st Battle Group, 23rd Infantry Regiment, was soon to embark on Exercise Willow Freeze. A camouflage scheme of sprayed white or light-colored paint was applied in stripes and zig-zags to the vehicle. A light-colored circle with a dark triangle in it, probably a tactical sign, was on the side of the gun mount and the front hull door. **Top right:** This M42 belonging to Combat Support, 1st Battle Group, 9th Infantry, from Fort Wainwright, Alaska, was photographed during Exercise Great Bear near Quartz Lake, Alaska, on 20 February 1962. A coating of white camouflage paint with hard edges has been applied to parts of the vehicle and is carefully cut in around the unit marking on the glacis. The vehicle and even the crewmen's arctic hats wear a tactical symbol of a white circle with dark-col-

ored triangle. **Above left and right:** An M42, registration number 12D326, was photographed between Crosswind and Fish Lakes, Alaska, during Operation Willow Freeze on February 17, 1961. The vehicle is in the same sprayed-white camouflage scheme as the earlier photo of an M42 of the 1st Battle Group, 23rd Infantry, and has the same foldable Plexiglas windshield with side wings. Snow is piled up here and there on the vehicle. (NARA, all)

In wintry conditions, an M42 crew of the 42nd AAA conducts live-firing exercises. The vehicle is wearing its stock semigloss olive drab paint scheme, with no attempt to camouflage it to match the snowy conditions. The barrels are not equipped with any flash suppressors and a crewman on the ground is ready to hand up a four-round clip of 40mm ammunition. "CPL BALLER" is painted in white on the side of the gun mount. A five-gallon liquid container is stowed in the rack to the front of the ammunition locker and there is an unusual set of very long turnbuckle eye bolts on the front towing shackles typical of the tie-downs used to secure the vehicles to railroad flatcars. Another M42 sits in the background. (Air Defense Artillery Museum)

In a photograph possibly taken at the same time and place as the preceding one, the crew of M42 U.S. Army registration number 12B746 performs a live-firing exercise in the winter. On the rear deck is a signalman with a white helmet cover, waving a flag. Next to him is likely the squad leader, the commander of the vehicle and crew. Note the absence of a flash suppressor on the visible 40mm gun barrel. (NARA)

U.S. Army mechanics perform maintenance or repairs on an M42. The mount is swung to the rear, and the barrels have been removed from the 40mm guns, the openings of which have been covered with tape. With the access doors of the rear deck open, the white-colored cross drive CD-500-3 transmission inside the rear of the hull is visible. (NARA)

Top left: Trainees are learning how to operate the M42 at the Air Defense School at Fort Bliss, Texas, on June 17, 1966. They were attached to B Battery, 1st Training Battalion. This M42 and the one parked next to it are coated with a fine film of dust, with rubbed-away spots especially on the equipment lockers below the ammunition lockers. The observers typically seen on the rear decks of M42s during live-firing exercises, one with a flag and the other on the phone, are present.

Top right: An M42 crew of the 1st Battalion, 44th Artillery, practices firing at an aerial target over the Doña Ana Range near Fort Bliss. The lids of several of the ammunition lockers to the side of the gun mount are open, since during firing operations it was necessary to retrieve ammunition clips from them on a continual basis. **Above left:** Major General George T. Powers III, commander of Fort Bliss, pauses to visit with Staff Sgt. A. M. Myers at the driver's controls of an M42 of B Battery, 1st Battalion, 1st AD GM Brigade on 17 February 1966. This is a later M42, as it lacks the split overhead door between the driver's and commander's hatches. The coil spring that assists in the opening and closing of the driver's hatch door is visible, as is the locking handle with a round knob on the end. **Above right:** Officer candidates learn the fine points of the gun mount of an M42 at Fort Bliss, Texas, on 25 July 1966. The front hull door is open, exhibiting the national insignia and bridge classification symbol. Spare 40mm barrels are stored under the ammunition locker and two antenna masts mounted on AB-15/GR mast bases are visible on the gunners' shields. (NARA, all)

In a posed photograph apparently taken during a training exercise or tests, the crew of an M42 stands at the ready in the gun mount, which is traversed to the rear. The vehicle's U.S. Army serial number, 12D089, is painted in white on the side of the right front 40mm ammunition storage compartment. The white object to the front of that number is the squad leader's periscope on his open hatch cover. The side stowage lockers are equipped with padlocks. Veterans report that the use of these padlocks was especially important in Vietnam to prevent pilfering by the civilian populace.(Rock Island Arsenal Museum)

Top left: During a training exercise for M42 crews at Fort Bliss on 30 June 1966, 1st Sgt. Richard E. Evans of Headquarters Detachment, 1st Training Battalion, Air Defense (AD), 1st Training Brigade (AD), demonstrates how easy it is to lob a hand grenade into the open gun mount. The results could be disastrous. This is the first of several photos taken on that occasion to document the benefits of a grenade catcher designed for the gun mount. **Top right:** Crewmen of C Battery, 1st Training Battalion (AD) are mounting an experimental grenade catcher over the gun mount of a different M42 on the same occasion at Fort Bliss. The grenade catcher was a tubular frame covered with mesh screen, with an opening at the front to accommodate the twin 40mm guns. **Above left:** The grenade catcher is in place, and the crewmen are demonstrating the hinged panels that allowed the crew to access the mount. An instructor at the left lectures a group on the device. **Above right:** The grenade catcher was intended to protect the crew from enemy hand grenades when the vehicle was in active combat zones. Although a well-meaning concept, it was one that did not take root, and grenade catchers were seldom if ever employed operationally. (NARA, all)

The staff sergeant to the right appears to be instructing the two specialists on some point concerning the 40mm Bofors gun system on M42 registration number 40228315. The vehicle is in new condition, with clean, semigloss olive drab paint and non-corroded mufflers, exhausts, and muffler shields. The three-piece cleaning rod stored in brackets on the side of the ammunition locker partially covers the national insignia. Radio antennas and their bases have not been installed. (Air Defense Artillery Museum)

An M42A1 Duster, registration number 12H298, was photographed in a sandy flats at Fort Bliss, Texas. This training vehicle is shorn of its radio antennas, flash suppressors, and defensive machine guns. The stencil at the front of the ammunition locker identifies a radio harness kit that has been installed in the vehicle. The small insignia on the mount and ammunition locker is that of the U.S. Army Air Defense Artillery Center and School. (Air Defense Artillery Museum)

Top left: A Marine crew with all eyes forward operates M42 USMC serial number 208900 at what appears to be a desert training base. On the storage compartment is a shield-type insignia with "1/AWS" on it. To the front of the gunner's face is the sight-accessory case.

Above left: The same M42, USMC 208900, is now deployed with the mount traversed to the left. The design of the gun shield, when viewed from the front or rear, provided scant protection to the crew, but was designed to offer protection to the gun receivers, the automatic loaders, and other vulnerable parts of the gun and accessories. **Right:** Marine crewmen of another M42, USMC 208926, place canvas muzzle covers over the flash suppressors of the 40mm guns. The vehicle apparently was nicknamed for Gen. Archibald Henderson, the 19th-century USMC commandant known to all Marines as the "Grand Old Man of the Marine Corps." Below the nickname is a "1/AWS" insignia. (NARA, all)

A U.S. Army M42, U.S.A. number 12G075, exits a landing craft upon crossing a river in the Republic of Vietnam. Markings on the lower front hull plate indicate the vehicle was assigned to 1st Battalion, 44th Artillery (Automatic Weapon, Self-Propelled), I Field Force Vietnam. Ring sights are visible on both sides of the gun mount. The box-shaped device on the right side of the shield is an antenna matching unit. (NARA)

When the Duster was upgraded with the fuel-injected Continental AOSI-895-5 engine, replacing the original Continental AOS-395-5 engine of the M42, the modified version was designated the M42A1. This example of an M42A1, registration number 40228548, served with the 4th Battalion, 60th Artillery, and was performing a defensive role at a fire-support base in Dak To Province during Operation Greely in July 1967. Worthy of notice are the non-reinforced, three-prong flash suppressors on the 40mm guns and the T141-style mudguards. (NARA)

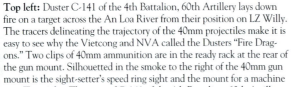

Top left: Duster C-141 of the 4th Battalion, 60th Artillery lays down fire on a target across the An Loa River from their position on LZ Willy. The tracers delineating the trajectory of the 40mm projectiles make it is easy to see why the Vietcong and NVA called the Dusters "Fire Dragons." Two clips of 40mm ammunition are in the ready rack at the rear of the gun mount. Silhouetted in the smoke to the right of the 40mm gun mount is the sight-setter's speed ring sight and the mount for a machine gun. **Top right:** The crew of C-141 of the 4th Battalion, 60th Artillery performs maintenance on their 40mm gun mount after a fire mission at Landing Zone Willy, Binh Dinh Province, Republic of Vietnam, on 19 July 1967. The twin-40s of the M42, which was in a sandbagged revetment, had been directing harassing fire at enemy units attempting to move through the entrance to the An Lao Valley. (NARA, two) **Above left:** The cover of one of the exterior 40mm ammunition storage compartments is open, revealing the contents. These compartments on both sides of the vehicle held a total of 240 rounds of ammunition in 60

clips. In addition, there were storage provisions inside the hull for an additional 240 rounds of 40mm ammunition, stowed in 16-round cans. (National Dusters, Quads and Searchlights Association) **Above right:** Sergeant Henry B. Hood, a squad leader of an M42, and SP/4 Delbert Benjamin, a gunner, both of B Battery, 4th Battalion, 60th Artillery, attached to the 173rd Airborne Brigade, feed 40mm ammunition clips into the automatic loader of their guns. They were in Dak To Province, Republic of Vietnam, performing crew drills in preparation for Operation Greely on 15 July 1967. (NARA)

Left: Two cannoneers from B Battery, 4th Battalion, 60th Artillery, load the 40mm guns of their M42A1 at the aptly named Duster Hill adjacent to LZ Uplift near Qui Nhon, Republic of Vietnam, on August 8, 1967. They were SP/4 Nick Carter (left) and PFC Tim Adcock. The M42A1 is emplaced in a sandbagged revetment in the perimeter defenses of the hill.
Right: At Landing Zone Willy overlooking the entrance to the An Lao Valley on 18 or 19

July 1967, PFC Wilson J. Burgett of North Hollywood, California, loads a 16-round 40mm ammunition can into M42 C-141 as part of the provisions for the vehicle's internal ammunition storage. In the background, a CH-47A Chinook helicopter is airlifting supplies into the landing zone. (NARA, both)

Top left: M42 crews of the 1st Battalion 44th Artillery stand for inspection at Camp J.J. Carroll with the Battalion Commander shaking hands with a crewman. On the right gunner's shield's of these vehicles is a housing of thin, welded steel to give some protection to the antenna matching unit MX-2799/VRC, a type of converter that was attached to the bottom of the antenna base and linked to the AN/VRC-46 radio set that set was installed in later-production M42s. (NARA)

Top right: Two M42s of the 1st Battalion 44th Artillery were photographed at the Rockpile (Position #1). The crew of the track on the left (A-122, RN: 12V319) is on a convoy run from Dong Ha, which indicates that Rt. 9 was open at the time. They appear ready for a sudden firefight, having filled the ready racks with 40mm ammunition and draped four-round clips over the side of the gun mount. A rear-pointing M60 machine gun and ammunition box are on the pintle mount at the rear of the 40mm gun mount. The unmanned M42 to the right, C-221 has the front hull door open and the twin 40s traversed to the rear. (Air Defense Artillery Museum) **Above left:** Two M42s of the 1st Battalion 44th Artillery stand watch behind a

sandbagged revetment. The location is Gio Linh (or Con Thien) overlooking the Ben Hai River valley and the DMZ. The front hull door is open on the closer vehicle. A piece of canvas is draped over the machine gun at the rear of the 40mm gun mount. M42s were frequently called on to provide perimeter defense at bases in Vietnam, a task they were well suited to with their powerful, fast-firing guns. (Air Defense Artillery Museum) **Above right:** Twin revetments were used by established Duster positions at LZ Action, a major base. This type of revetment was used so that the enemy would be uncertain of the actual Duster positions at night. With the guns facing over the engine deck, the Dusters were typically backed into the revetment, facilitating quickly moving the vehicle to another hotspot on the perimeter if necessary, and the engine and transmission provided a measure of extra protection to the crew. (Richard Fejfar via National Dusters, Quads and Searchlights Association)

Top left: An M42 of Delta Battery, 5th Battalion 2nd Artillery proceeds down a dirt road in 1969 while another advances cautiously through tall grass somewhere in III Corps Vietnam. Both vehicles have artwork on the front hull doors. The one on the right (RN: 12G226) has paintings of a scantily clad woman and a rabbit's head in profile, and "Twin Forty" written on it. The names of the track commander and driver are painted in white on the glacis. The track in the background has The Green Monster and artwork on the front hatch. **Top right:** The exposed nature of the gun crew of an M42 is evident in this view of a vehicle making its way through thick brush. The squad leader, or commander, is sitting above his hatch, wearing a CVC helmet (equipped with headphones and a microphone) so he can communicate with the crew and other elements. The driver has his head up through his hatch for better visibility. Two of four crewmen visible are in the gun mount. **Above left:** M42s advance abreast through a defoliated thicket. The crewmen are wearing flak vests to give them a bit more protection in their exposed mounts. The unit markings on the M42 to the right identify it as belonging to First Platoon, Third Section, Delta Battery, 5th Battalion, 2nd Artillery. Note the different location of the stars on the rear decks of the two vehicles. **Above right:** An M42 was photographed against the skyline with the lead setter, or right cannoneer, sitting at the ready behind an M60 machine gun. Two other crewmen sit on the ammunition ready racks, which provided a more comfortable place to perch than the thin wall of the 40mm gun mount. In the background, an OH-6 Cayuse "Loach" helicopter scouts the terrain for the enemy. (Air Defense Artillery Museum, all)

In a position called Duster Hill overlooking LZ Uplift, an M42 of 4th Battalion, 60th Artillery rests in an emplacement that has been dug out of a hillside. For any artillery system to achieve maximum accuracy, it is necessary to level the piece as accurately as possible. However, the M42 did not have a built-in mechanism for leveling the 40mm gun mount. Thus, for accurate firing, especially indirect firing, it was necessary to park the vehicle on as level a piece of ground as possible. (NARA)

Two M42A1s with Battery A, 5th Battalion, 2nd Artillery, stand by in the battery's motor pool at Tan Uyen, Republic of Vietnam, in mid-August 1967. A waterproof cover is strapped to the 40mm gun mount of the closer vehicle. On the fender to the front of the ammunition locker is an extra stowage box. The second M42 has its gun mount rotated to the rear. These M42s were engaged in perimeter defense and convoy escort. (NARA)

5th BATTALION AW (SP)
2ND ARTILLERY

A BATTERY
MOTOR POOL

Specialist 4th Class Jorge Fuentes, a gunner with Battery A, 5th Battalion, 29th Artillery, prepares to clean the barrel of one of the 40mm guns from his M42A1 at Tan Uyen in mid-August 1967. On the near end of the barrel are the interrupted screw threads that made for the quick removal of the barrel from the gun's receiver. Just beyond the interrupted threads is the coil spring of the recuperator mechanism. A gun barrel carrier tool sits on the left front support and a breechblock and firing pin components sit on the back left support. A roll of steel wool is also present. To the left is a new track that will replace one from one of the unit's M42A1s. (NARA)

In mid-August 1967, two members of Battery A, 5th Battalion, 2nd Artillery, motor pool put their muscles to removing the track from a M42A1. In an arrangement often seen on M42s in 5/2d tracks, an equipment rack made of iron c-bars and wooden slats has been installed on the rear of the vehicle. Webbing belts reinforce this version of the rear rack. Among the items stowed there are a mud-splattered cot and a 5-gallon liquid container. (NARA)

Left: In the defensive perimeter at Con Thien, Republic of Vietnam, in late July 1967, the driver of an M42A1 of Battery B, 1st Battalion, 44th Artillery, attached to the 3rd Marine Division, eases the vehicle into a revetment. The registry number, 12P397, appears on the front door. The flash suppressors have been removed from the muzzles of the 40mm guns. This was a common practice in Vietnam because the non-reinforced three-prong flash suppressors issued to many Dusters didn't hold up under steady use and were removed. **Right:** Three M42s were photographed at the Phu Thu Race Track near Cholon, Republic of Vietnam, on 9 February 1968, at the height of the Tet Offensive. The vehicles belonged to Battery B, 5th Battalion, 2nd Artillery, attached to the 25th Infantry Division. Clips of 40mm ammunition are draped over any available spot on the gun mounts, in readiness for sudden sustained firing. Trailers are coupled to each of the M42s; the two closest ones appear to be M104 or M105 1 1/2-ton trailers. No auxiliary generator mufflers are visible on these units. (NARA, both)

Duster C-141, registration number 40228536, with the Battery C, 4th Battalion, 60th Artillery, works in cooperation with the 1st Platoon, D Company, 1st Battalion, 8th Infantry, during a search and sweep mission near Qui Nhon, Republic of Vietnam, on 9 August 1967. The vehicle retains one of the two boxes on the rear deck for M20 3.5" antitank rockets. A dust cover is arranged over the pintle-mounted machine gun on the rear of the 40mm gun mount and an ammunition box is sticking out from under it. The canvas turret cover is bundled and stowed on the deck behind the turret. (NARA)

During preparations for Operation Greely on July 15, 1967, PFC Charles W. Abbott, a photographer with Department of the Army SP Photo Team C, films movie footage of the gunner of an M42A1 of the 4th Bn 60th ADA near Dak To. The gunner's speed ring sight and smaller rear peep sight are visible. The case on the rear of the shield to the front of the gunner is the gun sight accessory chest M61, in which was stored the speed ring sights, reflex sight M24C, and other gun sight fixtures. Rather than stenciled white signs indicating the location of stowed gear, this vehicle has yellow signs with black and white borders and black lettering. (NARA)

At Camp Rock Crusher, near the base of Black Virgin Mountain, this M42A1 from 5/2d ADA was set up to aid in perimeter defense around August 16, 1967. As was often the case in defensive scenarios, the gun mount is rotated to the rear. "GYPSY" is painted on the gun shield in yellow. A binocular case is strapped to the right antenna base, and below it is the flash suppressor removal tool. A M60 machine gun is in the pintle mount. Ammunition boxes for the M60 are strapped to the rear of the gun mount. (NARA)

In July 1967 during the middle period of Operation Pershing, an eleven-month-long search-and-destroy operation in the An Lao Valley, 1st Lt. Albert Carden indicates to squad leader SP/4 Phillip A. Pettice where he wants the M42A1 in the background to lay down a concentration of fire. The vehicle, registration number 40228536, belonged to the 4th Battalion, 60th Artillery. On the M42A1, the crewman with the helmet loads a 40mm ammunition clip into the ready rack. A small Confederate flag is on the antenna. In Vietnam, mud was virtually omnipresent on vehicles in the field. (NARA)

Lt. Albert Carden waves M42 C-142 into a firing position at Landing Zone Willy, adjacent to the entrance to the An Lau Valley, during Operation Pershing on July 18 or 19, 1967. The driver was identified as SP/4 Larry G. Womack. Mud obscures all of the unit markings on the front of the hull. (NARA)

The crew of Duster A-48 of A Battery, 5th Battalion, 2nd Air Defense Artillery Regiment, is on alert during a pause in the action in the summer of 1967. The driver and the squad leader, standing in the hatches, are wearing CVC helmets, while the crewman next to the M60 machine gun on the right side of the mount is using a headphones/microphone set over his M1 helmet. Coming up behind is another M42, apparently A-49. (Roland Rodi via National Dusters, Quads and Searchlights Association)

An M42A1 pulls into a perimeter-defense position at Landing Zone Two Bits, near My Lai (4), Republic of Vietnam, on August 9, 1967. The vehicle was with C Battery, 4th Battalion, 60th Artillery. Bits of gear are strapped to footman loops on the ammunition locker. One of the crewmen has put his flak vest to good use as a seat cushion. The light gray boxes to the left are storage chests for 40mm ammunition. This vehicle has the early-style squared fenders at the front. (NARA)

Details of the housing on the front of the right gunner's shield for the antenna matching unit necessary for the AN/VRC-46 radio are visible on track C-142 of 4/60th Artillery moving up to its assigned emplacement at Landing Zone Willy during Operation Pershing in July 1967. On the track is a typically diverse Duster crew (L to R): cannoneer SP4 Ralph Widener, holding his M-16; standing in the TC hatch without a helmet is SSG Billy D. Titus; in the background wearing the helmet with goggles is cannoneer PFC Johnson; the driver is SP4 James Womack; sitting on the driver hatch cover is Sgt Carrol Flemister; behind him is PFC Richard Tyler in the gunner's position. (NARA)

The crew of an M42A1 of B Battery, 4th Battalion, 60th Artillery, scrambles to their stations during a crew drill during Operation Greely, July 16, 1967. A 5-gallon liquid container is stowed at the front of the ammunition locker, and a host of gear is fastened to the vehicle, from canteens and ammunition holders to knapsacks and musette bags. One crewmember uses the road wheel and upper track to make it up to the turret. When traversing up and over the rear muffler one has to account for whether it is hot or not. (NARA)

With helmets and flak jackets on, the crew of this Duster providing perimeter defense are on alert. The muzzles and automatic loaders of the guns as well as the machine gun on the far side of the 40mm gun mount are well covered to keep dust out. A 40mm ammunition storage container is sitting on the ground to the front of the hull to serve as a step up to the driver's compartment. Lying on the roof of the hull next to the driver's hatch is a pair of binoculars, while several shaving kits and an empty C-ration box are among the piled-up tarps sacks of empty sandbags and equipment in the foreground. (Air Defense Artillery Museum)

An M42 crew is preparing to fire at a target in the lower terrain to the left. For such firing situations, the 40mm guns could be depressed up to -5 degrees under manual operation, or -3 degrees under powered operation. All three doors of the ammunition locker are open, exhibiting their embossed ribbing, and several 40mm clips are propped up in the locker for quick access. A full clip of four rounds of ammunition is visible in the automatic loader. The storage boxes for M20 3.5" rockets are visible on the rear of the M42 to the left. The vehicle at the rear is fitted with the storage boxes for the M20 3.5" bazooka, as well. (Air Defense Artillery Museum)

While the twin Bofors of M42 registration number 12V291 are being fired at a target in the low ground ahead, one of the cannoneers is kneeling down to grab a 40mm ammunition clip from the locker. The locker lid is leaning on a five-gallon liquid container resting on the fender. In the area below the ammunition locker, to the rear of the spare 40mm gun barrels is another five-gallon liquid container resting on its side, with its handles visible. (Air Defense Artillery Museum)

The left cannoneer is retrieving a clip of 40mm ammunition from the ready rack, while the right cannoneer is preparing to insert a clip into the automatic loader. Loading was accomplished by positioning the clip into the guides of the automatic loader and pushing the clip downward until the bottom round dropped into the loader tray. (Air Defense Artillery Museum)

Duster crews of Battery A, 5th Battalion, 2nd Artillery, work to make sure their gun mounts are ready for their next mission, in the Republic of Vietnam, in 1967. The nearest vehicle is U.S. Army serial number 40228158. Below that serial number, the door of the forward storage bin is missing, with some crumpling to the bin being visible. (NARA)

At a Landing Zone Willy in the Republic of Vietnam in July 1967, an M42 of the 4th BN 60th Artillery assigned to the 41st Artillery Group is entrenched behind sandbags, covering the entrance to the An Lao Valley and ready to lend support when needed to the 1st Battalion, 7th Cavalry Regiment, during Operation Pershing, a search-and-destroy mission in the valley. To the right is an M151 MUTT from B-Battery 29th Artillery (SLT) with a xenon searchlight mounted in the rear who were attached to the 4/60th. (NARA)

Top left: A Duster situated in a perimeter defense emplacement bears an odd assortment of extra gear. In addition to two five-gallon liquid containers strapped to the ammunition locker, a 55-gallon steel drum that has been cut in half is lying on the spare-track rack: a prize the crew may have picked up for use as a fire/BBQ pit or wash tub. In view on the transmission cover are the boxes for the 3.5" rockets and the infantry telephone. (Air Defense Artillery Museum) **Top right:** Specialist 4th Class Larry G. Womack checks the oil of his M42 at Landing Zone Willy during Operation Pershing in the An Lau Valley in mid-July 1967. Womack was the driver of this vehicle, C-142. The pintle-mounted machine gun is carefully wrapped, and hanging over the side of the 40mm gun mount is a flak jacket. At the far right is an infantry telephone box. A flight of helicopters passes overhead. (NARA) **Above left:** The crew of an M42 in Vietnam poses on the deck of their vehicle. The flash suppressors have been removed from the muzzles of the guns, and two

C-ration boxes dated 1967 are strapped down next to a five-gallon liquid container. The hinges of the lids of the ammunition locker are visible; these were fairly light-duty contrivances made of steel wire bent into rectangles and retained by hinge leaves on the lid and the side of the locker. **Above right:** The sight of the gun mount of an M42 rising above its revetment would have given pause to NVA or Vietcong sappers contemplating assaulting the perimeter of a base camp. Stacked on the embankment to the front of the mount are the ubiquitous 40mm ammunition storage containers. (Air Defense Artillery Museum, two)

A crewman peeks around a tent while an M42 12B845 sits in an adjacent revetment. Crewmen have tracked mud all over the lids of the ammunition lockers, and a waterproof cover protects the automatic loaders of the 40mm guns from the dampness. The crew has cleverly used opened C-ration cans to cover the tips of the 40mm cannons to keep out the dirt. Stacked on the other side of the vehicle are 40mm ammunition containers. (Air Defense Artillery Museum)

In a field in Vietnam adjacent to a ruined building, two M42s are deployed with their guns traversed to the rear in support of infantry operations. Notice the slight tilt of the track of the nearer vehicle, caused by the torque of the drive sprockets. Smoke is visible exiting the vehicle exhausts as it moves cross-country. All of the left ammunition locker doors are open. The closest vehicle's guns lack flash suppressors, while the other Duster has them installed. (Air Defense Artillery Museum)

A combat photographer captured this view of an M42 of Alpha Battery 1st Battalion, 44th Artillery, passing a truck somewhere in Vietnam. Five-gallon liquid containers are stashed on both fenders, and an M60 machine gun on the pintle mount at the rear of the 40mm gun mount is pointing straight at the photographer. The commander and a crewman in the gun mount are wearing CVC helmets, but an M1 helmet, possibly the commander's, is wedged against the rear of the right headlights. (Air Defense Artillery Museum)

Left: 2nd Platoon Leader, 1LT Bruce Geiger of Alpha Battery 1st Bn, 44th Arty, in a flak vest hefts a 40mm ammunition container in front of A-242 at FSB A3 between Con Thien and Gio Linh, Feb 1968. Soon after this, Lt. Geiger would be choppered under-fire into Khe Sanh Marine Base to take command of the Duster and Quad-50 sections defending the base from ground assaults. In March, under Operation Pegasus, a relief column entered the base was headed by Dusters from Charlie Battery 1/44th ADA. They would stay there protecting the base until it was dismantled around June 18, 1968. (Air Defense Artillery Museum) **Top right:** An M42 crew from 1st Platoon Charlie Battery 4th Bn, 60th Arty, conducts a sweep of the An Lau Valley in April 1967 in support of the 1st Battalion, 7th Cavalry of the 1st Cavalry Division in Operation Pershing. The vehicle's registration number on the front hull door

was 40228544. Reinforced three-prong flash suppressors are affixed to the muzzles of the 40mm guns. **Above right:** At the airstrip at Landing Zone Two Bits, an M42, registration number 40228536, was photographed on April 15, 1967, during Operation Pershing. The vehicle was with C Battery, 4th Battalion, 60th Artillery, attached to the 1st Cavalry Division. In the unit markings on the front of the hull, IFFV stands for I Field Force, Vietnam; 4 is the battalion; AW is Automatic Weapons; 60 is the regiment; C is the battery; and 141 is the vehicle number. (NARA, two)

These two Dusters belonged to the 5th Battalion, 2nd Artillery in Vietnam. The front M42 has vehicular art on the front hull door: a white silhouette of a shapely woman with "DREAM–" lettered below it. A form-fitting waterproof cover is strapped over the gun mount, with openings in it allowing the radio antennas to remain in place. (Patton Museum)

"DREAM–" is viewed from a different angle. Two different styles of front mudguards are on this vehicle, both with squared fronts. The left mudguard has lateral ribs and a support and is of the style found on the T141, while the right mud guard appears to have been fabricated from smooth sheet metal. By contrast, the Duster to the rear has the later mudguards with the angled fronts. (Patton Museum)

Mud and glare have obscured the 40228548 registration number of this Bravo Battery 4th Bn, 60th Arty Duster photographed on July 15, 1967, during Operation Greely. The stenciled name "FOX" is clearly visible on the glacis to the front of the commander's hatch. The driver is in his seat with his head above the hatch and is wearing a CVC helmet. Neither of the hatch doors has a periscope installed in the periscope mount. The flash suppressors on the 40mm guns are the three-prong, non-reinforced type. This vehicle has the early-style squared fenders at the front, as well as the overhead doors between the hatches. (Patton Museum)

In order to alleviate some of the exposure to enemy fire of the crewman operating the M60 machine gun in the side pintle mount, an improvised shield was installed on this Duster. Visible over the right headlights is the bridge classification sign, signifying 23 tons. A water cooler, essential gear in hot, humid Vietnam, is on the front fender of this Duster in the 5th Battalion 2nd Artillery motor pool area. (Patton Museum)

The crew of the same M42 shown in the preceding photo, registration number 40228594, tends to their vehicle at a motor park in Vietnam. Stowed on top of the improvised stake rack at the rear of the Duster are several five-gallon liquid containers along with other equipment. The rear of the machine gun shield is visible to the left of the man standing to the right on the Duster. (Patton Museum)

Top left: Another M42 in a 5/2d Arty motor pool in Vietnam in June 1968 has a similar stake rack at the rear, but the horizontal slats are fewer in number than those in the preceding photo, and appear to be of 2x6 lumber. A crosspiece through the vehicle's lifting eyes holds the rack in place. The crewman to the right is opening the equipment locker that held spare parts and tools for the 40mm guns. **Top right:** An M42 from A Battery, 5th Battalion, 2nd Artillery, sits in a vehicle park in June 1968. The front hull door is open, providing a glimpse of a 40mm ammunition container stored between the driver's and commander's seats. The antenna mount on the left gun shield is a later, boxy type, as contrasted with the early, cylindrical type. Spent 40mm rounds along the rim of the turret were used for make riding seats for the gunner and azimuth tracker. **Above left:** This surprisingly clean M42

is emblazoned with numerous markings. The vehicle was C-112 with C Battery, 5th Battalion, 2nd Artillery, and was photographed in a sandbagged revetment in Vietnam a half mile from the Cambodian border. The name "Have Guns Will Travel" was a play on the title of a popular TV Western. **Above right:** The crew of this Duster of B Battery, 60th Artillery, are prepared for the sustained pounding of a target near the Cambodian border on August 14, 1967, with ready rounds arrayed around the rear of the gun mount and the ammunition locker lids swung open. The gunner has set his helmet on one of the wooden poles set up to hold a sunscreen and is wearing headphones for intercommunications. The staff sergeant observing the weapons' fire at the right is probably the vehicle section chief. (Patton Museum, all)

This M42A1 from the 2nd Platoon, Battery B, 4th Battalion, 60th Artillery, was emplaced to guard a bridge on QL14 north of Pleiku between Camp Enari at Dak To and Kom Tum City, March 27, 1968. Faintly visible are the hinges for the two-panel overhead door between the commander's and driver's hatches, marking this as an early-production vehicle. A U.S. flag flies from the antenna for the AN/VRC-46 radio set. (NARA)

Part of the escort for a convoy in the Republic of Vietnam is this M42 Duster (C-112, registration number 12P369) assigned to C Battery, 1st Battalion, 44th Artillery (Automatic Weapon, Self-Propelled). A canvas dust cover is over the M60 machine gun on the right side of the mount. The shield over the twin 40mm guns has a distinctive white stripe painted on it. Caked-on dirt and mud was the norm on vehicles in Vietnam. It was rare to see one in shiny, clean condition. This vehicle also has the early-style squared fenders at the front, as well as the overhead doors between the hatches. This Duster is marked with the USARV command designation (not IFFV or XXIV GP) 1AW44. (NARA)

Top left: An M42A1 (C-231) test fires at the range beyond the perimeter of Camp Enari, near Pleiku, Republic of Vietnam, on March 25, 1968. The Duster was with Battery D, 4th Battalion, 60th Artillery, assigned to the 4th Infantry Division. On the antenna is a blue flag with small stars. Visible on the right side of the transmission cover is the infantry telephone box. A small star insignia is at the center of the middle door of the equipment lockers. (NARA) **Top right:** Crewmen of a Duster stand sentry in a perimeter defensive revetment. An M60 machine gun and ammo box are mounted on the side pintle mount. Only one radio antenna is mounted: the type AT-912/VRC, on an AB-719/VRC antenna base support. This antenna was linked to the AN/VRC-46 radio set, a radio/intercom system that included an RT-524/VRC FM transmitter-receiver for voice signals between vehicles. The antenna for the AN/GRR-5 shortwave receiver, which enabled the Duster to monitor communications, is not installed. (NARA) **Above left:** A Duster from Bravo Battery 4th BN 60th Arty (B-242) stirs up dust on a road in a base camp in Vietnam. The area is fairly secure, and the crewmen are not wearing helmets or flak vests. An illegible inscription is painted in white letters on the front of the 40mm gun mount. (US Army Transportation Museum) **Above right:** Automotive repair trainees at the U.S. Army Ordnance Center and School, Aberdeen, Maryland, examine the power pack of an M42 or M42A1 in the background. The engine, with an aluminum-colored block, is on the left, and the white transmission is partially visible to the right. The black object at the top of the engine is the engine oil cooler. The transmission oil cooler is at the top of the opposite side of the engine. The Continental AOS-895-3 engine used in the M42 was replaced by the Continental AOSI-895-5 in the M42A1. (NARA)

Dusters are undergoing maintenance in the Alpha Battery 5th Bn 2nd Arty motor pool 1970-71. The Duster to the left of the front row appears to have an ACAV-style armored shield added to the right-side machine gun mount. A power pack is sitting on the ground in front of the Duster to the right of the 2-1/2 ton 6x6 truck. None of the 40mm Bofors guns are fitted with flash suppressors. (Jack Ryan via NDQSA)

An M42 crosses a pontoon bridge next to a highway bridge that may not have been sturdy enough to bear the weight of armored or heavy vehicles. The markings at the top of the glacis are mostly hidden by gear. A skull is painted on the gun shield. In the foreground is a guard post evidently manned by ARVN troops. (Air Defense Artillery Museum)

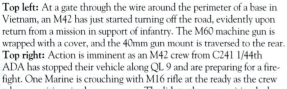

Top left: At a gate through the wire around the perimeter of a base in Vietnam, an M42 has just started turning off the road, evidently upon return from a mission in support of infantry. The M60 machine gun is wrapped with a cover, and the 40mm gun mount is traversed to the rear.

Top right: Action is imminent as an M42 crew from C241 1/44th ADA has stopped their vehicle along QL 9 and are preparing for a fire-fight. One Marine is crouching with M16 rifle at the ready as the crew take up positions in the gun mount. The lids to the ammunition lockers are open, and ready clips of 40mm ammunition are in place around the mount. The soldier to the right on the deck appears to be an infantryman who left his M16 leaning against the vehicle and is about to indicate to the gun crew where to direct their fire. To the right on the roadway are several spent 40mm shells indicating that the Duster has already returned fire against the enemy. (Air Defense Artillery Museum, two) **Above left:** A M42A1 of the 4th Battalion, 60th Artillery, is in a strong point position commanding Route 14 in the An Khe pass west of An Khe, Republic of Vietnam on 16 June 1969. The 40mm gun mount is traversed to the rear,

and the lid of the forward ammunition locker is open. One of the crewmen is supplementing the 40mm guns' fire by taking a shot with his M16 rifle. The Squad Leader appears to be on the radio, (NARA) **Above right:** An M42A1 from Charlie Battery 1/44th ADA, returns to its home base with several "hitch-hikers" after being detailed to a fire-support base near Minh Long, Quang Ngai Province, June 26, 1971. By this time, the U.S. Army began withdrawing its Duster-equipped air-defense artillery units from Vietnam. Painted on the gun shield of this vehicle is "WENDY'S HELL GUNS", and the XXIV marking on the front of the hull refers to the XXIV Corps. (NARA)

Top left: Behind a revetment topped with 40mm ammunition containers sits an M42 from C Battery, 4th Battalion, 60th Artillery at Fire Support Base Beaver, 12 kilometers northwest of Bong Song, April 1, 1970. The visible crewmen were listed as, left to right, PFC Donald A. Hanshaw, azimuth tracker; Sgt. Thomas C. Blanford, squad leader/loader; and SP/4 Michael A. Tribur, gunner. "DANGER HIGH VOLTAGE" is hand-lettered on the right antenna mount. **Top right:** A study in concentration: the crew of this Duster gun mount have focused their attention to the front. The automatic loaders of the guns are full, and the loaders stand poised to insert additional clips into them. Refueling hoses with screw couplings are strapped to the rear of the gun mount. **Above left:** Specialist 4th Class Floyd William of Baytown, Texas, buffs the inside of the front door of M42 Duster B-111 with the markings of Battery B, 4th Battalion 60th Artillery at Fire Support Base Black Hawk in

September 1970. At least eighteen full clips of 40mm ammunition can be seen hanging on the gun mount. The front hinges and the hold-open latch of the overhead hatch of the early M42 are visible at the top center of the glacis. (NARA, three) **Above right:** As an unseen crewman prepares to hand off another four-round clip, SP4 Theodore "Bill" Twardy (left) and SP4 Gerald Johnson (right), cannoneers, feed automatic loaders of the guns of track B-232 "Twin 40's" in late 1971. Shot at the firing range next to Dragon Mountain south of Pleiku where Camp Enari was once located, these were some of the last Duster rounds fired by Americans in Vietnam. To load a clip into the gun, the cannoneer positioned the loaded clip into the guides of the automatic loader and then firmly pushed the clipped rounds down until the bottom cartridge dropped into the loader tray. (Richard Fejfar via National Dusters, Quads and Searchlights Association)

Top left: Trainees are working toward Military Occupational Specialty (MOS) 16F—light air defense artillery crewmember—at the Air Defense School, Fort Bliss, Texas, in 1969. In Vietnam, the enemy knew that when the M42's guns were in this position (during maintenance) they could not fire. There were instances when crews were told not to do routine maintenance because the enemy would then take that opportunity to fire on the bases. (NARA) **Top right:** Second Platoon Leader 1LT Vincent Boyle (on left) B-4/60 ADA oversees crewmen prepare to pull a 40mm Dual Automatic Gun M21 from an M42 Duster at a base camp near Kontum in 1971. The barrels, the recoil cylinders, and the trunnion caps securing the gun to the mount have been removed, the receivers have been elevated to 90 degrees, and the piece is ready to be hoisted free. **Above left:** The twin 40mm gun receiver assembly has been pulled free from its mount. The battery's gun mechanic in the foreground has his hand on the elevating sector, which is not on the centerline of the bottom of the receivers but rather centered on the bottom of the left receiver. **Above right:** With the 40mm dual gun assembly removed, the inner parts of the Mount M4E1 are visible, as seen from the rear of the mount. Inside the mount are mechanisms for elevating, traversing, and firing the 40mm guns. To the far left is the storage case for sight accessories, and to the far right is a holder for a binoculars case. In the background, lying on the rear deck of the vehicle, are the two 40mm gun barrels. (National Dusters, Quads and Searchlights Association, three)

Top left: The crews of two M42 Dusters with the 5th Battalion, 2nd Artillery pause for a break in a town in the Republic of Vietnam. The M42 to the front is U.S.A. number 40228280, while the other one is 12D633. A refueling hose is strapped to the side of the ammunition compartments on the leading M42. **Top right:** The crew of Duster A121 of A Battery, 5th Battalion, 2nd Artillery, dismounts. Written on the hull door is "Roaring Dusters Forties," while the names of the driver, PFC Shortnancy, and the squad leader, SGT Dunlap, are marked on the top of the glacis. Like A121, once an entire platoon bore "Dusters Roaring Forties" door markings. A red fire extinguisher is secured with a clamp to the fender. **Above left:** Near Pleiku RVN; Second Platoon leader of B- 4/60 ADA, 1LT Vincent Boyle discusses with squad leader Sgt John Korzek (in wet fatigues) how Duster B-232 rolled down into a creek in June 1971. The vehicle had just been washed nearby when the brakes failed. After recovery of the vehicle will come the rigorous chore of thoroughly draining and cleaning it, then restoring the electrical and mechanical systems. Barely visible on the top of the filter and ductwork are the words "NO STEP" in white paint. Everyone that worked atop a Duster had to remember not to step on these fragile components. **Above right:** The last remaining members of the 4/60th ADA are cleaning Duster B-112 in December 1971 in preparation for turning it over to the ARVN. South Vietnam would maintain a Duster battalion of their own starting in 1972 using the operational tracks from the three deactivating US Duster battalions. This vehicle has a red caution on the side of the antenna matching unit reading "HI / VOLTAGE." (National Dusters, Quads and Searchlights Association, all)

During mid October 1971, a memorial service was held at Weigt-Davis base south of Pleiku, RVN. This service was for PFC Gary Mizner (IL) of B Battery, 4th Battalion, 60th Artillery who died on 5 October 1971 of the plague. He was the last known Duster casualty of the Vietnam War. He served on Duster B-131 "The Ones" seen here. Note the early square fender design and the straight T-Bar steering handle. Later models would have a curved steering handle. The light-colored object on the base for the right headlights appears to be a Buick sticker, probably placed there by a fan of that company in the crew. (Richard Fejfar BCO via National Dusters, Quads and Searchlights Association)

Top left: Top left: The crew of M42 (B-132 RN: 12D087) "George of the Jungle" pose for their portrait. Across the front door is the sign that hung on 1st Platoon's bunker at Weigt-Davis compound, reading: "YOU'RE IN THE HANDS OF DUSTER DEATH." The speed ring sight is nicely visible as is the small oval "BUICK" sticker below the left side light. Driver, Roger Whisenant sports goggles and "boonie" hats have long replaced the standard stateside ball-caps. **Top right:** The two M42s in the preceding photo are seen from the rear along with two other M42s on a firing line in Vietnam. The lawn chair is present on the second vehicle. The firing appears to be fast and furious, with the cannoneers keeping busy loading the guns from the stocks of ammunition stacked on the rear decks and clipped to the mount. **Above left:** An M42 crewman takes a cigarette break in a makeshift hammock strung from steel fence stakes wedged into the side of U.S.A. number 12C295 at a fire-support base in the Central Highlands of the Republic of Vietnam. Duster crews were on call day and night and got their rest whenever the opportunity happened. Atop the 40mm ammunition storage compartment is a field phone. **Above right:** A fire devastated the engine compartment of this M42 Duster as viewed from the rear. The once white transmission assembly in the foreground is now a charred gray color. Jutting from the upper left of the transmission is the engine-oil-filler tube with its cap missing. To the left of the tube is the left engine-exhaust line. (National Dusters, Quads and Searchlights Association, all)

A wrecker crane is being employed to hoist the power pack of an M42 Duster using a specially designed T-bar bracket that properly suspends the powerpack. Track mechanic Sgt Andy Hutchins of B-4/60th ADA uses hand signals to guide the crane operator. Track squad leader SGT James Throckmorton observes from above. He sports an unofficial in-country made patch of 4/60th Dusters on his shirt pocket. The white transmission and the dark-colored engine were constructed so as to be able to be installed or removed as a single assembly. On the center of the side of the engine are three rocker valve covers; above them is the transmission oil cooler. On the right side of the engine, above the rocker valve covers is the engine oil cooler. (National Dusters, Quads and Searchlights Association)

Top left: Replacement new and depot-overhauled engines were shipped in sealed, nitrogen-charged steel canisters. Such an engine is seen here, with the upper half of the canister lifted away in preparation of installing the engine in a 1st Platoon B-4/60 ADA Duster at Weigt-Davis engineer's compound south of Pleiku, RVN, during fall 1971. **Above left:** A M543-series wrecker crane has lifted the engine from its container, and it will soon be mated with the new transmission, which is resting on 40mm ammunition containers. Visible in the lower half of the engine can are desiccant bags. (Richard Fejfar BCO via National Dusters, Quads and Searchlights Association, two) **Right:** In a twin 40mm gun mount of an M42 Duster, the gunner sits to the right of the photo while the two cannoneers to the rear stand ready with additional clips of ammo to be loaded in the guns. The gunner's helmet cover has his home state Delaware and the word "SHORT" indicating that he is getting close to going home. The projectiles' coloration, green with a white ring and a red tip, indicates the type, HE-T-SD: high-explosive, tracer, self-destroying fuse. Despite their brassy appearance, the 40mm shell casings are not brass, but made of steel. (NARA)

Squad Leader Sgt. Duane Schewe walks by B-132 (registration number 12D987) "George of the Jungle," a 4th Battalion, 60th Artillery M42 Duster in a sandbagged revetment at Position 4, Weigt-Davis Fire Support Base, south of Pleiku, in June 1971. The mount is traversed to the rear, with the rear deck of the hull just visible above the sandbags. A barrel-cleaning staff lies on the deck. The forward parts of the 40mm gun barrels appear dark, probably from a fresh coat of oil. Barrels were rarely painted, as the paint would burn off during firing and leave a residue. On the antenna are, top to bottom, a small U.S. flag; a black memorial flag, and a yellow flag recognizing this vehicle's total of kills, 58. (National Dusters, Quads and Searchlights Association)

Members of the 1st Battalion, 44th Artillery, survey battle damage to an M42 Duster in Vietnam. The rear doors have been completely blown off the rear deck, and several louvered doors are askew. A badly damaged three-forked flash suppressor is present on the right 40mm barrel but no flash suppressor is present on the left barrel. Visible discoloration of the paint indicates that a significant fire had engulfed the vehicle. The right track is also missing, and there appears to be damage to the sprocket. (Larry Ross via National Dusters, Quads and Searchlights Association)

Duster C-231 of the 5th Battalion, 2nd Artillery, has lost its left drive sprocket and track, leaving it stranded in the mud. In 1970, the entire platoon adopted the "Have Guns Will Travel" artwork on the hull door, which was named after a popular Western TV series; the "white knight" paladin symbol referred to the main character of the show. The last name of SP/4 Thomas Robertson is painted to the front of driver's hatch. Automatic-loader lifting tools are hanging from below the rear machine-gun pintle. (National Dusters, Quads and Searchlights Association)

The first vehicle in a row of M42s, U.S.A. number 40228158, of A Battery, 5th Battalion, 2nd Artillery, is undergoing repairs to its left compensating idler wheel and front road-wheel suspension. Two track pins and nuts sit atop one of the stacked road wheels in the foreground. Lying on the tarpaulin in the right foreground is a long pry bar. Numerous machine-gun ammunition boxes are stored on the fender below the ammunition compartments and a fuel transfer hose is strapped to the mount. All the Dusters in the line have the canvas turret cover attached. (National Dusters, Quads and Searchlights Association)

Top left: An M42 Duster of A Battery, 5th Battalion, 2nd Artillery is being refueled from a tanker truck. Duster battalions strived to maintain their own fuel trucks to support themselves in the field. Note the improvised stowage rack on the rear of the M42 and the trailer hitched to it to the far left. **Top right:** A soldier motions the driver of M42 B-111 of the 4th Battalion, 60th Artillery, aboard a trailer on the route to Lane Army Airfield in the Republic of Vietnam as the Battalion prepares to deactivate in December 1971. With the exception of a muddy hull bottom, the M42 is in unusually clean condition for a Vietnam AFV, with the unit markings showing clearly. The tow hooks are painted white. **Above left:** M-42 Duster C-131 of the 5th Battalion, 2nd Artillery, is on a landing craft at a river crossing in the Republic of Vietnam. The nickname "The Collector" is painted in Gothic script on

the gun shield. Two Duster crewmen in flak vests are standing to the sides of the mount. In Vietnam, 5/2d and 4/60 Dusters did perform actual firings from LCMs and even did actual test landings and recoveries back to the LCMs where feasible. **Above right:** To provide fire support in otherwise impassible terrain around the Mekong Delta, an M42 Duster is parked on a pontoon raft that is being propelled by the landing craft, mechanized (LCM) to the right. The front and rear of the raft is heavily fortified with bunkers made of sandbags. Cyclone fencing for anti-rocket defense is rigged on the sides of the raft; the name "Buttercup" decorates the closer fencing. In the foreground are two PBRs (Patrol Boats, River). (National Dusters, Quads and Searchlights Association, all)

Top left: If ever a military site was aptly named, it was Landing Zone Mud, north of Pleiku, Republic of Vietnam, in 1971, as the crew of this M42, B Battery 4th Battalion, 60th Artillery, could attest. Torrential rains had inundated this landing zone, leaving the Duster deeply mired. The driver is seated in the vehicle, attempting to start the engine, but the chances of the vehicle exiting the morass under its own power appear to be slim. **Above left:** An M42 Duster, B-111 of the 4th Battalion, 60th Artillery, U.S.A. number 12B911, occupies a defensive position at Landing Zone Action near Mang Yang Pass in mid-1971. The vehicle was backed into the revetment, for rapid egress if necessary. No flash suppressors, one antenna, tow cable and cleaning rods visible. Tarpaulins cover the guns, automatic loaders, and clips of 40mm ammunition fastened to the rear of the mount. A metal clip extractor tool draped across the mount rim just behind the lifting loop. Just beyond the M42 is an ammunition bunker, and in the

right background are an ACAV M113 personnel carrier and an M48 tank with a xenon searchlight. **Right:** A likeness of the Zig-Zag Man and the motto "Can Do" decorate the hull door of M42 Duster C-111, U.S.A. number 12C295, of the 4th Battalion, 60th Artillery, at a camp in the Central Highlands of the Republic of Vietnam in mid-1971. A crewman takes a snooze on a folding cot in front of the Duster. Duster crews were on call 24-7 x 365. Getting any rest, even in the middle of the day, was important to the mission. An M16 rifle leans against the mount, and personal gear is in abundance on the vehicle. For the crew's comfort, several folding chairs are on the vehicle. (National Dusters, Quads and Searchlights Association, all)

An M42 Duster of A Battery, 5th Battalion, 2nd Artillery, stands guard on a dusty road in Vietnam, overseeing the recovery of a jeep that went off the road and into a canal. The squad leader or track commander is kneeling over his hatch, apparently speaking into the microphone of his CVC helmet. Only one antenna is mounted on the gun shield. The track has not been personalized with any artwork at this time and the gun's openings have ration cans over them to keep dirt out of the barrels. (NARA)

Left: In early 1968, M42 Dusters of the 1st Battalion, 44th Artillery, engaged in street fighting during the Battle of Hue. These vehicles conducted hit-and-run attacks on enemy positions; darting out into a street, blasting the position with 40mm fire, and retiring just as quickly. Here, one of the 1/44 Dusters makes its way along a street, with plentiful 40mm rounds at the ready on the rim of the mount and the crewmen hunkered down in the open mount. (NARA) **Top right:** After the Vietnam War, Dusters continued to serve for over a decade with the National Guard as well as with the armed forces of several other nations. This example is painted in a MERDC (Mobility Equipment Research and Development Command) four-color camouflage scheme developed by the U.S. Army in the early 1970s. Although this scheme largely comprises light colors, the white areas prescribed for snowy areas are not present. (Air Defense Artillery Museum) **Above right:** This Duster exhibits the MERDC camouflage scheme commonly found on U.S. military vehicles through the mid-1980s. Much of the paint is flaking off, exposing the underlying olive drab color. In addition, the tracks are rusty from neglect and the rubber shoes of the tracks are severely deteriorated. (Department of Defense)

In mid-1968 a Duster from the 1st Battalion 44th Artillery caught fire and burned off during a refueling mishap (hot engine) out at a firing range at Dong Ha Base Camp, Quang Tri Province. The damage from the gasoline fire and cooked-off 40mm rounds was so extensive that not even the guns or computing sight were salvaged. Rather, the Duster was left at the range as a gunnery and small arms target. Note the downward extension of the left fender under where the side 40mm ammo was stored. The rubber has burned off the road and idler wheels as well as the track pads. At the center of the hull is the open lid of the rear ammunition locker. (Air Defense Artillery Museum)

A number of M42 Dusters survive in the United States and several foreign countries. This beautifully restored example is owned and restored by the National Museum of Americans in Wartime. It is in a plain Olive Drab paint scheme and is marked with U.S. Army registration number 12C126. Fitted on the 40mm gun muzzles are three-pronged flash suppressors with a reinforcing band. (Scott Taylor)

Top left: With the hull door open, a glimpse into the interior of this restored M42A1 is available. On the far right side of the opening, parts of the driver's seat and his curved steering-control crossbar. The white, cross-shaped object toward the bottom of the opening is the range-selector control lever. **Top right:** This front door of the hull is the late-production type, with a bracket for a flashlight, a .30-caliber ammunition stowage box, a large box for an M19 infrared periscope with a smaller box for a spare periscope head on it, and a bracket for an electrical diagram. These doors on early-production vehicles were less cluttered and lacked the periscope box. **Above left:** Looking through the front door, to the right is the driver's seat, and to the left is the squad leader's seat. Dominating the rear of the driver's

compartment is the personnel heater. The gasoline-burning heater, rated at 20,000 BTU per hour, is mounted on a support plate, below which are the exhaust tube, the fuel pump, and the fuel filter. Above the heater is a rack for storing four rockets for defensive use. **Above right:** As seen through the front door of an M42A1 with the squad leader's seat to the left, an Olive Drab heater duct runs from the rear to the front of the compartment. A flex hose, missing here, connected the heater to the rear end of the heat duct. The white mechanism next to and below the rear of the heat duct is the parking brake assembly. The white loop-shaped object above the duct is the guard for the primer pump handle.

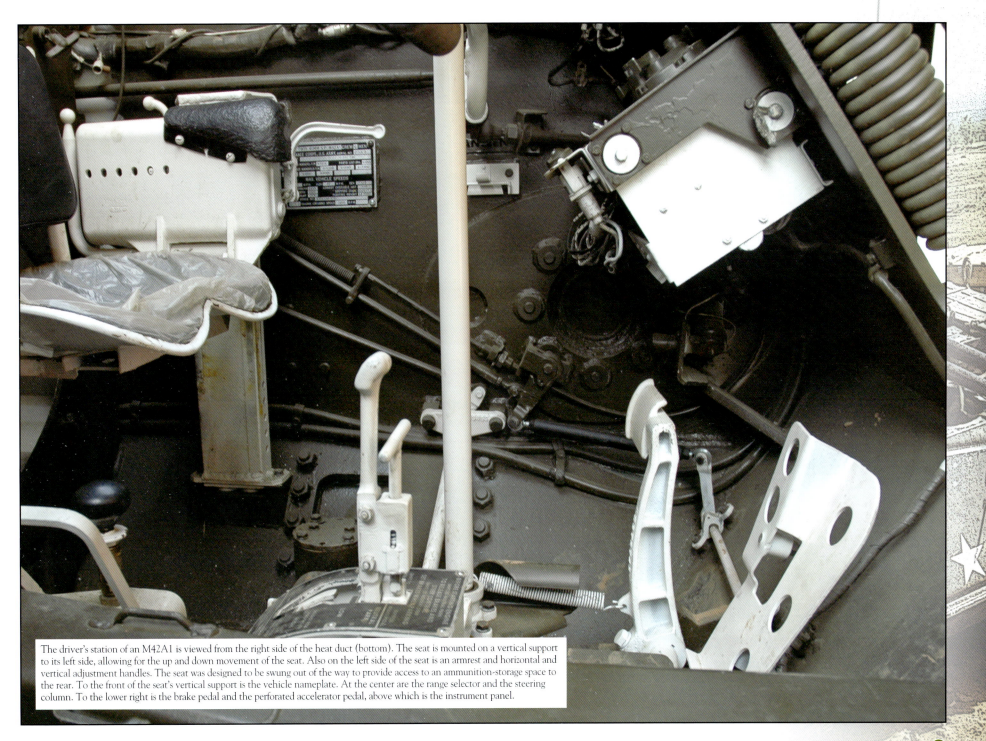

The driver's station of an M42A1 is viewed from the right side of the heat duct (bottom). The seat is mounted on a vertical support to its left side, allowing for the up and down movement of the seat. Also on the left side of the seat is an armrest and horizontal and vertical adjustment handles. The seat was designed to be swung out of the way to provide access to an ammunition-storage space to the rear. To the front of the seat's vertical support is the vehicle nameplate. At the center are the range selector and the steering column. To the lower right is the brake pedal and the perforated accelerator pedal, above which is the instrument panel.

Top left: The instrument panel is seen with the steering control in the foreground. To the left of the panel is the blackout selector switch. On the top tier of the instrument panel are, left to right, the light switch assembly, the warning light panel, and (hidden) the starter, magneto, booster, and degasser switch assembly. The gauges on the bottom tier are, left to right, the left fuel tank gauge, right fuel tank gauge, and (hidden by steering column) engine-oil pressure gauge. **Top right:** To the right is the bearing bracket on which the top of the steering control column pivots. Attached to the left side of the steering crossbar is the steering link. To the left of the bracket are the auxiliary generator and engine control box and a small panel holding the speedometer/odometer (left) and the tachometer (right). Partially visible above the speedometer is the driver's dome light. **Above left:** The driver's station in an M42A1 is seen from above, with the front of the hull to the

right. At the top right is the coil-spring assist for the hatch. To the left, behind a curved armor guard, is the external handle for the fixed interior fire extinguisher. **Above right:** The range-selector control box and handle are seen from above. On the control box is a plate with instructions on the proper use of the selector. The range-selector is used to set the driving ranges of the selective-gear trains, from high to low to reverse. To the rear of the selector is the primer-pump handle and its loop-shaped guard.

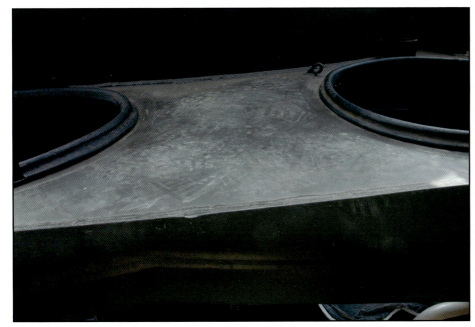

Top left: By comparison with the preceding photo of the solid roof above the driver's compartment, this image shows an early-production Duster with a front and a rear overhead door between the driver's and the squad leader's hatches. The purpose of this door was to facilitate handing 40mm ammunition stored inside the hull, up to the 40mm gum mount. The front panel was hinged at the front, and the rear panel at the rear, with the seam between the two panels running between the inboard parts of the two hatches. **Top right:** As seen from the inside of an early Duster facing to the rear, the front and rear overhead doors between the top hatches was supported by a longitudinal bar, which also acted as a surface to which the two door latches were engaged. The support bar was pivot-mounted on its front end, allowing it to be swung out of the way when the door was opened. Below the rear overhead door are the driver's and commander's radio/intercom control boxes.

Above left: A view of the roof of the driver's and squad leader's compartment facing to the rear illustrates the solid plate in lieu of overhead doors that was characteristic of the late-production Dusters. Surrounding the hatch openings are rubber weather seals with cutouts on the inboard portions to provide clearance for the hatch locks. **Above right:** The upper hull plate of the later production vehicles was plain armor plate, devoid of the levers and seam required in the early design.

Top left: The squad leader's seat is shown secured in its normal position. The seat could be raised and lowered on its support using the curved handle on the outboard side of the seat. The top of the support is secured to a bracket with a pull-pin, visible between the two seat-back cushions. To the left are racks for radio equipment. The white object next to the M1 carbine is the oil-bath filter for the auxiliary generator and engine. **Top right:** The squad leader's compartment is viewed facing right. On the bottom rack are a speaker, left, and an amplifier power supply, right. The caution sign to the top relates to reinstalling drain-hole covers after draining water from the hull. **Above left:** As viewed through the front door of the hull, a gray-colored 16-round 40mm ammunition can is in the storage space to the rear of the squad leader's seat, shown here tilted out of the way. There was one of these spaces, referred to as tunnels, on each side of the hull. Six cans of ammunition were stored in each tunnel. **Above right:** The right ammunition-storage tunnel is shown empty of 40mm ammunition cans. To the left of the sign indicating the location for storing rations is the air duct from the auxiliary generator and engine air cleaner to the auxiliary generator and engine in the rear of the hull. To the upper right is the personnel heater. At lower left can be seen the fuel tank selector, left tank, right tank, both, off.

Top left: This vehicle has late-type headlight groups, characterized by a humped brush guard to provide clearance for a horn at the top of the right group and a blackout driving light at the top of the left group. Shown here is the right headlight group, comprising, left to right, a blackout marker lamp, a service headlight, and a blackout headlight. Missing is the horn above the headlights. Early-type headlight groups lacked the horn and the blackout driving light, and the tops of the brush guards were straight. **Top right:** In a view of the upper right hull front and part of the 40mm gun mount, the squad leader's hatch cover is closed, showing the periscope objective and its brush guard. Also on the hatch cover is a handle. Toward the left are an armored bin for 30-caliber ammunition, welded to the gun mount, and a stored five-gallon liquid container. **Above left:** The interior of the squad leader's open hatch cover is seen from the side, facing inboard. In the foreground is the lock handle. Beyond the lock is the periscope; either the M13 or M13B1 periscope was provided to the squad leader and the driver, with the driver also having an M19 infrared periscope for night driving. The periscope is mounted on a holder called the adapter, which allowed for rotating and tilting the periscope. **Above right:** In a closer view of the squad leader's periscope, on the face of the adapter is a knob for securing the periscope in the adapter. On the side of the adapter is a small knob for locking the angle of the periscope, which had an elevation range of 25 degrees. On the turntable is a knurled knob for locking the azimuth of the periscope.

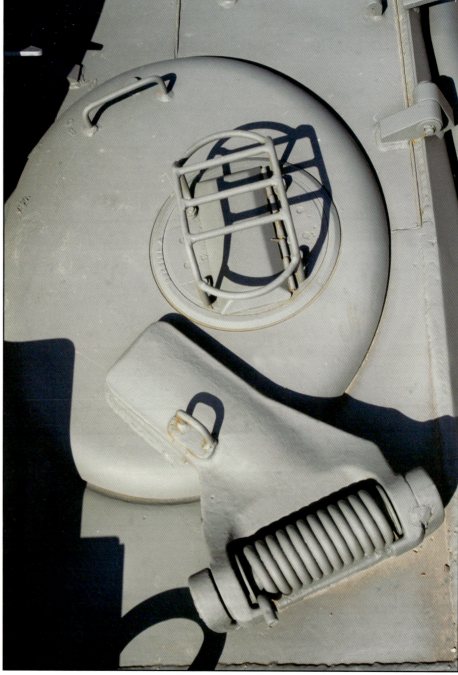

Left: The squad leader's seat is seen through his open hatch. This is a late-production Duster, lacking the two overhead doors between the hatches. To the bottom right is the coil spring assist for the hatch cover. To the bottom left is the armored bin for carrying .30-caliber ammunition. **Right:** The squad leader's hatch is closed on an early-production Duster equipped with overhead doors between the two top hatches. To the right of the photo are the right hinge and the hold-open latch for the front overhead door. The design of the top of the periscope brush guard is shown. A small lifting ring is welded to the hinge arm of the hatch cover.

A restored M42A1 Duster is observed from the right side with the 40mm gun mount traversed to the rear and the bow door and hatches open. The Duster had five sets of road wheels, or bogie wheels, per side. The suspension was of the torsion-bar type, and the torsion bar arms for the first two wheels and the rear wheel were fitted with shock absorbers. (Scott Taylor)

Above the right fender is a structure containing 40mm ammunition compartments on top and storage compartments for tools and equipment on the bottom. On the side of the ammunition compartments is a tow cable, one eye of which is secured to a holder in the foreground. Farther to the rear on the side of the ammo compartment is a holder containing three sections of a bore-cleaning staff.

US ARMY 12H224

Top left: In a detail photo of the right storage compartments, the design of the tow-cable holders is visible at the upper center. Basically, they were a bent piece of steel that used the cable's weight to keep it in place. Above the cable are hinges for the forward ammunition storage compartment cover. Below the cable is the forward storage compartment door, with recessed T-shaped lock handles. **Top right:** Red mud is caked on the right track of a Duster in a photo emphasizing the front track-support roller assembly, one of three on each side of the hull. These rollers were fitted with solid rubber tires, as were the road wheels. The mounting bracket for the track-support roller in the foreground has a steel guard that is welded to the hull, whereas the center roller's mounting bracket lacks this feature. **Above left:** The bore-cleaner staff for the 40mm guns is stowed in three sections on the side of the right ammunition compartments. The three sections screw together to form a single staff. Above the staff are two tow-cable holders. Above, on the side of the 40mm gun mount, numerous footman loops are provided for attaching crew knapsacks. The bracket for the forward pintle

mount for a machine gun is to the upper right. To the rear of the gun mount is a ready rack for clipped 40mm ammunition, with a holder on the side for a canteen. The objects that look like grab handles on the ready rack are actually holders for a pouch containing asbestos mittens. **Above right:** Above the right fender, between the muffler, left, and the rear of the stowage compartments is the right oil-bath air filter, for purifying air before it is inducted into the carburetor. Stamped on the cup on the bottom of the filter is an oil-fill line. Next to the filter is a clamp that holds the tow-cable eye in place. A feature of the curved parts of the 40mm gun shield was dimpling of the surface, faintly visible in this view at the top right.

The general arrangement of the right muffler, pioneer tool rack above the muffler, oil-bath air filter, drive sprocket, and other features is displayed in this view of an M42A1. The box inboard of the exhaust tailpipe is a telephone box that allowed troops outside of the vehicle to communicate with crew or to access the vehicle's radio.

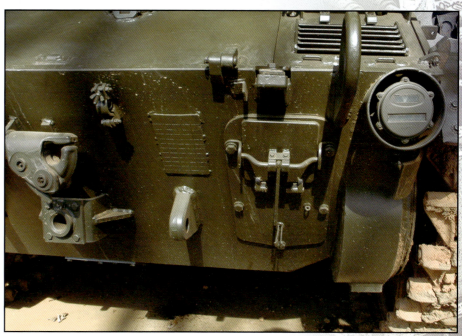

Top left: The right oil-bath air cleaner is seen close-up. It is attached with clamping bands to the plate at the rear of the storage compartments. The oil pan at the bottom of the filter is secured with a steel cable attached to a sprung latch, visible here. To the side of the air cleaner is the tow-cable clamp. **Top right:** The mufflers of the Duster are enclosed in boxy heat shields with angled upper facets. The right one and the tailpipe (far left) are pictured. Straddling the front and rear of the muffler are steel brackets that support the pioneer tool rack. The mattock handle and the shovel are visible from this angle. Mounted on the inboard side of the rack is the muffler for the auxiliary generator and engine. **Above left:** The pioneer tool rack, its rear bracket, and the muffler and tailpipe are seen from the rear. Attached to the tailpipe with a U-bolt clamp is an exhaust deflector that points upward. Next to the muffler is the exterior telephone and radio/intercom box. Details of the rear of the fender also are in view. **Above right:** On the rear plate of the hull inboard of the right tail light and lifting eye is a plate with a small waterproof door on it, fitted with a locking mechanism. This was the access for two features: the original C-980/U intercom control for the use of support troops and personnel outside of the vehicle, and the electrical connections for a towed trailer or for off-vehicle use. To the left are the stowed pintle hook and, below it, its mounting bracket.

The layout of the rear of the Duster is displayed with the 40mm gun mount traversed to the rear. From this angle, the air ducts attached to the air cleaners are visible. Connected to each air cleaner are separate air inlet and outlet ducts. On the rear deck to the front of the lifting eyes is the transmission-access door. To the right of center on the upper part of the cover is the door for the transmission oil filler. On each side of this door is a louvered battery-access door.

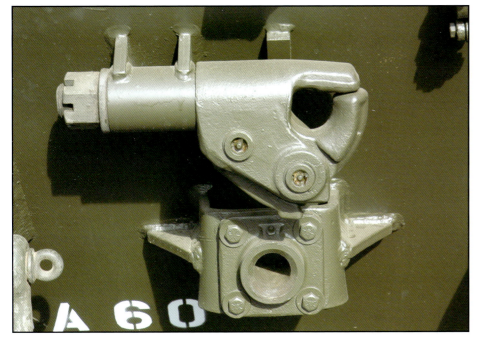

Top left: The door on the right rear of the hull for the intercom box and electrical receptacle has two hinges on the bottom and is secured firmly in place by a latch comprising a handle and a lateral curved rod that engages a lug on the hull to each side of the door. To the lower right, inboard of the track, is the final drive adapter, with a plate containing the drain plug on the bottom of it. **Top right:** Another detail shot of the rear of the hull shows the stowed pintle hook with, below it, its mounting bracket, and above and to the right the clamp-type holder for the pry bar. To the far left side of the hull above the final-drive adapter is the holder for the business end of the pry bar. **Above left:** The pintle hook is in its stored position, with its shaft secured in a cylindrical holder welded to the hull. The same locking nut and washer that would lock the pintle hook into its mounting bracket, is used here to secure the hook in its holder. **Above right:** The left final drive adapter is seen close-up, revealing the double weld beads on its inboard facet and the single weld bead that fastens the adapter to the rear of the hull. The final drive adapter provided the necessary, armor-protected offset for installing the final-drive assembly.

Top left: The 40mm automatic dual gun M2A1 and its 40mm twin-gun mount M4E1 are traversed to the rear, as viewed over the rear deck of a Duster. On the curved part of the hull below the gun shield and above the rear deck, the bent-rod brackets were for holding the rolled-up gun-mount cover, with straps attached to the brackets and to the footman loops securing the cover in place. **Above left:** To the left is the left muffler, tail pipe, and exhaust deflector. On the tray above the left muffler were stored four spare track links, secured with

brackets; a gun-barrel carrier tool; two track-connecting fixtures; and a drift pin for driving track pins from track assemblies. Farther forward, on the inboard side of the air cleaner are the air inlet (top: squared shape) and air outlet (bottom: round shape) ducts. **Right:** The left taillight and lifting eye are shown. Both of the taillights were housed in armored guards. The left taillight assembly comprised a service taillight and service stop light over a blackout taillight. The right taillight assembly had a blackout stop light over a blackout taillight.

The general arrangement of the M42A1 Duster from the left rear is displayed. Unlike the storage compartments of the right side, with 40mm ammunition compartments located over compartments for tools and equipment, the left side of the vehicle featured 40mm ammunition compartments above a space for stowing spare 40mm gun barrels on the fender. (Scott Taylor)

US ARMY 12H224

On another restored Duster seen from the left side, the manner in which four brackets hold the left 40mm ammunition compartments well above the fender is apparent. In addition to the brackets at the front and the rear of the compartments, there are two more brackets in between.

Top left: The rear bracket of the left 40mm ammunition compartments is seen from a closer perspective, showing how the bracket also forms the rear face of the rear ammo compartment. A five-gallon liquid container is stored on its side below the compartment, to the rear of which is the left oil-bath air cleaner, muffler, and spare-tracks rack. **Top right:** There are three ammunition compartments per side, each with a cover with two hinges on the outboard side made of heavy-gauge wire; three of the hinges are visible here. On the side of the 40mm gun mount are ample footman loops for hanging crew combat packs. Stencils mark the locations for stowing two packs and a canteen. Also in view is the left 40mm ammo ready rack, with holders for a pouch for asbestos mittens, for handling hot barrels or spent cartridges. **Above left:** In the space for storing spare 40mm gun barrels are two muzzles with three-forked flash suppressors on them. These are late-type suppressors with a reinforcing rod around the forks. To the left is one of the support brackets for the ammunition compartments. **Above right:** In a longer shot of a different Duster, the spare 40mm gun muzzles are fitted with a type of plain, three-forked flash suppressor occasionally seen in photos of Dusters in the Vietnam War. The rack for the five-gallon liquid container, with an angle-iron retainer on the front end and a webbing retainer strap, is shown.

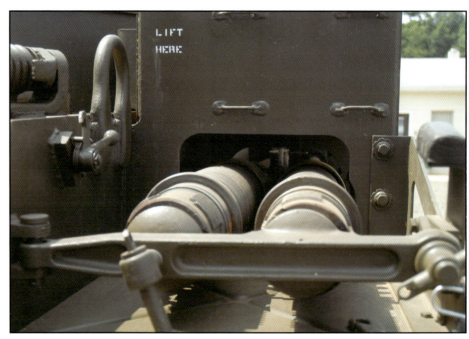

Top left: Footman loops are welded along the sides of the 40mm ammunition compartments. On the fender below the compartments is a rack for two spare 40mm gun barrels, in the shape of two troughs to conform to the shape of a barrel. Loops for webbing straps are on the rear part of the rack. Large, rounded openings in the two center support brackets for the ammo compartments provide clearance for the spare barrels. **Top right:** Toward the forward part of the spare-barrels rack are two barrel clamps. These comprise a toggling, curved clamp on one side of each of the troughs in the rack, and a T-shaped clamp nut on the other side. The chain acts as a retainer for the clamp nut. **Above left:** Two 40mm gun barrels are stored in the spare-barrels rack, rear ends toward the front of the rack, showing the recuperator springs and the brass-colored barrel guide sleeves. To the left, the forward support bracket for the 40mm ammunition compartments has an opening in it to allow space for the spare barrels. **Above right:** In addition to the straps on the muzzle ends of the spare gun barrels and the barrel clamps to the fronts of the recuperator springs, an end clamp for the breech ends of the spare barrels was provided. This consisted of a bar on a swivel mount with discs that fit against the muzzle ends of the barrels, and two screws with T-handles for tightening the clamp. Normally, a canvas cover was placed over the breech ends of the spare barrels before they were stored in the racks. Toward the left are the driver's hatch hold-down latch and the left front lifting eye.

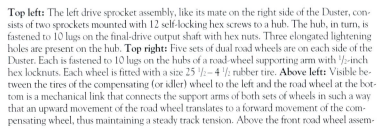

Top left: The left drive sprocket assembly, like its mate on the right side of the Duster, consists of two sprockets mounted with 12 self-locking hex screws to a hub. The hub, in turn, is fastened to 10 lugs on the final-drive output shaft with hex nuts. Three elongated lightening holes are present on the hub. **Top right:** Five sets of dual road wheels are on each side of the Duster. Each is fastened to 10 lugs on the hubs of a road-wheel supporting arm with $\frac{1}{2}$-inch hex locknuts. Each wheel is fitted with a size 25 $\frac{1}{2}$ – 4 $\frac{1}{2}$ rubber tire. **Above left:** Visible between the tires of the compensating (or idler) wheel to the left and the road wheel at the bottom is a mechanical link that connects the support arms of both sets of wheels in such a way that an upward movement of the road wheel translates to a forward movement of the compensating wheel, thus maintaining a steady track tension. Above the front road wheel assembly are, left to right, a bumper-stop spring to limit the upward travel of the road-wheel arm, and a shock absorber for the front road wheel. **Above right:** At the front of each track is a compensating wheel, or idler wheel, consisting of dual wheels mounted back to back. Like the road wheels and the track-support rollers, they are equipped with solid rubber tires and are the same size as those of the road wheels, 25 $\frac{1}{2}$ – 4 $\frac{1}{2}$.

Top left: A late-type left headlight group and brush guard is mounted on this Duster. It features a blackout driving light over, left to right, blackout headlight, a service headlight, and a blackout marker lamp, with a brush guard with a bulge on top to give clearance to the blackout driving light. To the left is the counterbalancing spring that assists in opening and closing the front door. **Top right:** The left headlight group is viewed from above. The light housings have rear and front elements that screw together to allow access to the light bulbs. At the center of the photo, positioned above the right brace of the brush guard, is the lever for the hold-open lock for the front door, to keep the door from inadvertently slamming shut when open. **Above left:** Like the squad leader's hatch cover discussed earlier, the driver's hatch cover is mounted on a arm connected to the hinge; on the hinge is

a coil spring that acts as a counterbalance to make it easier to raise and lower the hatch cover. A lifting ring is welded to the hatch arm. On the hatch is a turntable with the periscope cover and brush guard. **Above right:** The squad leader's hatch and open hatch cover are seen from above. Stored next to the hatch cover is a five-gallon liquid container. Also in view are the tow cable, the bin for machine gun ammunition, and the right headlight group and brush guard.

Top left: "Twin 40's" cartoon art is painted on the movable part of the gun shield of this Duster. A lifting eye is indicated by a stencil on the left side of the shield, above which is a mounting point for a radio antenna. On the opposite side of the shield is a shield for a matching unit for another antenna. A subtle, recessed waffle pattern was a standard feature of the fixed gun shield. **Top right:** The type of three-forked flash suppressor with the reinforcing rod around it is fitted on these Duster twin-forties. The purpose of the flash suppressor was to prevent the crew from being temporarily blinded by muzzle flash during nighttime firing, and also to reduce the piece's visibility to the enemy. **Above left:** The 40mm gun barrels where they exit from the armored shield are shown in this view of the gun mount traversed to the rear. The recuperator springs around the barrels are enclosed in housings, but the brass-colored barrel-guide sleeves at the fronts of the recuperator springs are exposed. **Above right:** In a view of the forward right portion of the 40mm gun mount from the side, the pintle mount for a machine gun is at the center. Behind the pintle mount is a lifting eye. Rising above the pintle mount on the shield is the shield for an antenna matching unit. To the left is an attachment point and stencil for a canteen.

In a view over the rear deck toward the gun mount with the twin 40mm guns traversed to the front, to each side of the rear machine gun pintle is a lifting eye. Several 40mm ammunition clips are in the left ready rack and draped over the gun mount.

Top left: Strapped to footman loops below the pintle mount are the two lifter implements that were used for removing the automatic loaders of the 40mm guns for inspection, repairs, or replacement. **Top right:** The left ready rack for clipped 40mm ammunition is seen close-up. The two ready racks were designed to hold two clips of ammunition. Also in view are the hanger for a canteen and the mounts for holding a pouch of asbestos mittens. **Above left:** During a firefight, the four clips of 40mm ammunition in the two ready racks would be expended very quickly, so crews tended to hang extra clips of ammo over the top of the gun-mount tub.

Above right: The front-right 40mm ammunition compartment is viewed looking down with the hinged cover open. Inside are dividers for 10 clips of ammo; at four rounds per clip, each of the six exterior 40mm ammo compartments could hold 40 rounds. To the front of the compartment (left) is a holder for a five-gallon liquid container.

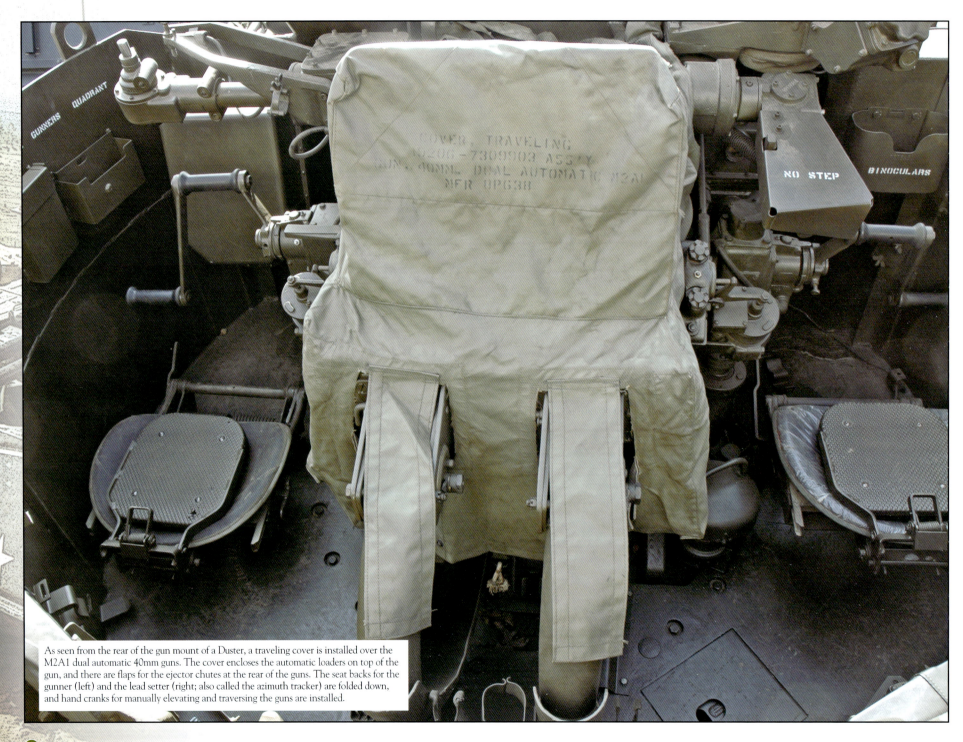

As seen from the rear of the gun mount of a Duster, a traveling cover is installed over the M2A1 dual automatic 40mm guns. The cover encloses the automatic loaders on top of the gun, and there are flaps for the ejector chutes at the rear of the guns. The seat backs for the gunner (left) and the lead setter (right; also called the azimuth tracker) are folded down, and hand cranks for manually elevating and traversing the guns are installed.

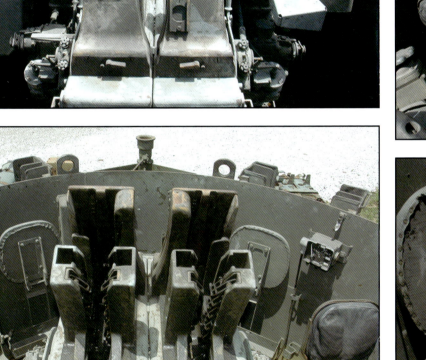

Top left: In a view of the 40mm gun mount of a Duster from the rear, the automatic loaders are in the foreground. Normally, a sight accessories case was stored on the rear of the left side of the shield. The dome-shaped mechanism to the rear of the right side of the shield is the M38 computing sight. This sight was used when tracking aircraft or moving vehicles. The lead setter manually set estimated target course and speed into the computer sight, which then calculated a firing solution. **Top right:** A Duster gun mount is viewed to the rear, with the automatic loaders of the 40mm guns at the center. On the rear of the mount are folding seats for the two cannoneers. Outboard of each seat is an intercom control box for the respective cannoneer. The structure running across the bottom of the photo is part of the M38 computing sight assembly and acts in part as a support for the computing sight mechanism (bottom left) as well as the speed-ring sights, peep sights, and the M24C reflex sight. **Above left:** In another view facing to the rear in a gun mount, at the center of each of the automatic loaders are two raised structures that contain the feed pawls and the stop pawls. To the front and the rear of the loaders are raised guides. Part of the autoloader is housed within the gun and includes a loader tray and a rammer. **Above right:** On each 40mm gun, on the right mounting bracket for the spent-case deflector is a fixture that looks like a compass scale but is actually a recoil indicator. It displays the length of recoil and includes a curved scale and an indicator arm. This one is on the left gun.

Top left: The body or casing of the dual 40mm gun to the rear of the barrels is referred to as the slide. The left half is designated the Mk. 1 and the right half is the Mk. 2. This view shows features on the Mk. 2 side. The curved handle on the right half of the photo is the right hand-operating lever, which is used to prepare the gun for firing. At the upper rear corner of the slide is a safety catch, for holding the hand-operating lever in the open position if desired. **Top right:** A dual 40mm gun mount is seen from the gunner's perspective. Below each of the spent-casing deflectors (right) is a curved chute for the spent casings. The mounting brackets for the movable shield at the front of the gun slide are visible toward the left, and the thickness of the shield can be seen. **Above left:** The M38 computing gun sight in a Duster is observed from the right side. The dome houses the computer. To the far left is the computer-positioning hand wheel, which rotates the computer in azimuth to match the estimated direction of flight of the target aircraft, to match the flight-

direction indicator on the bail above the dome. The round, black object with the studded face is the speed knob, for setting the estimated speed of the target. On the inner side of that knob is an angle-of-flight indicator. **Above right:** At the upper front of the right shield of a Duster is an armored shield for an antenna matching unit (not installed), a converter device. On top of this shield is a perforated plate for mounting an antenna base on. Bolted to the top of the right shield is a cushion, a standard fitting on the right shield but not the left shield.

Top left: The right interior of a gun mount is shown. The lead setter's seat back is folded down. A hand crank for manually traversing the mount is installed. On the other side of the mount, the gunner was equipped with a similar hand crank, but for manually elevating the guns. The dome-shaped object with a handle on the floor is the cover of the M27 azimuth indicator. Above it is the firing solenoid for the right gun. **Top right:** The M38 computing gun sight is seen close-up from the rear. The Black flight-direction indicator on the Olive Drab bail above the computer dome is visible, as is the small, red pointer for the angle-of-flight indicator on the inside of the speed knob. Below the computer is the traversing mechanism. **Above left:** In the front right portion of the gun mount, to the left of the binoculars holder, is the traversing mechanism of the mount, designated the azimuth oil gear M6A1E1. Oil gears that were controlled electrically powered the elevating and traversing mechanisms of the Duster's gun mount. **Above right:** As viewed from above the lead setter's seat, directly above the azimuth indicator cover is the right trunnion and trunnion cap. To the side of the trunnion is the firing solenoid for the right gun. The traversing hand crank is inserted in the traversing mechanism.

In a view to the right rear of the gun mount traversed to the rear towards from the driver's seat, between the two cannoneers' seats are, left to right: a cartridge extractor tool; stowage space for a jimmy bar; and a shell pusher, for freeing jammed 40mm rounds. On the floor next to the shell pusher is a box for grenades. Below each cannoneer's seat is a holder for a box of machine gun ammunition; the left one is visible here.

Top left: The tub of the gun mount comprises two stacked steel rings, welded together and reinforced with several stakes welded to the interior of the tub. The rear pintle mount for a machine gun is welded to three supports. Dangling from the pintle socket is a travel lock for a machine gun. **Top right:** The cannoneer's seats are made of painted plywood with up-holstering and are mounted on folding metal brackets. The left seat is shown. Adjacent to it is the left cannoneer's intercom control box. Above the box is a hook for hanging a telephone. **Above left:** The back of the gunner's folded seat back has a non-slip surface so it can be stood on. On the tub of the gun mount are holders for a firing table and a gunner's quadrant. The large, box-shaped object to the front of the manual-elevating crank is the

drive controller. When the guns were under operated under power control, the gunner used handgrips on the drive controller to elevate, traverse, and fire the guns. **Above right:** In an overhead view of the gunner's station, at the center of the photo to the front of the seat and the elevation hand crank is the left side of the M38 computing sight. The round object at the end of the shaft is the mount for the M24C reflex sight when used. When not in use, this sight was stored in the sight accessory chest at the top of the photo. The bar with the angled bend in it below that box is the open-sight bracket, which held the speed ring sight. The bent bar fastened to the M38 computing sight above the elevating hand crank is the mount for a peep sight.

Top left: The gunner's seat, like the lead setter's seat, had a spring-loaded backrest and was adjustable horizontally and vertically to suit the size of the occupant. The lever on the left side of the seat base is for vertical adjustment. Bolted to the floor to the right of the seat base is the elevating lock for the 40mm guns. It is in the locked position. **Top right:** The elevating mechanism is next to the left side of the 40mm gun carriage. At the upper center is the attachment point for the elevating hand crank for the manual elevation of the dual 40mm guns. In the left half of the photo is the M6A1E1 elevation oil gear for the powered elevation of the guns. **Above left:** A view from above the gunner's seat shows the relative positions of the sight accessory chest (top center); the left side of the M38 computing sight with the

mount for the M24C reflex sight; the brackets for the ring sight and the peep sight; the elevating hand crank; the left firing solenoid (bottom right); and the M12E2 drive controller, below the ring-sight bracket. The drive controller is in the stored position. For use, the bottom end was swung upward, making the hand controls available to the gunner. **Above right:** The speed ring sight is installed on its bracket, as viewed from the front of the mount. Whereas under power control the 40mm gun mount was operated using the drive controller in conjunction with the M48 reflex sight, under manual control the guns were operated with the hand cranks in conjunction with the ring sights. The ring sight was attached to its bracket with the two wing nuts seen here.

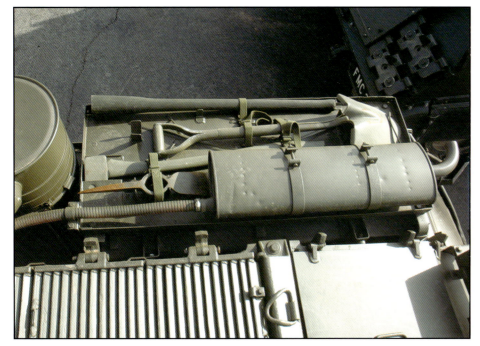

Top left: The rear deck of a Duster is viewed from above the right air cleaner with the gun mount traversed to the rear. In the foreground are the three panels of the engine-compartment grill. The center panel lifted off, while the outer panels were hinged on their outboard sides. To the rear of the grille is the front transmission-access door (center), flanked by the two front battery-access doors. **Top right:** The front right corner of the rear deck is viewed. A "NO STEP" stencil is on top of the air cleaner. At the center of the photo to the front of the grill is the exhaust shroud for the auxiliary generator and engine. Passing through the shroud en route to the small muffler on the pioneer tool rack is a flexible exhaust line. **Above left:** From left to right above the rear part of the right fender is the air cleaner and its air ducts; the pioneer tool rack; and the auxiliary generator and engine muffler and tailpipe. Running into the muffler is the flexible metal exhaust line. **Above right:** Secured with webbing straps in the pioneer tool rack are a standard complement of mattock head, mattock handle, shovel, and axe.

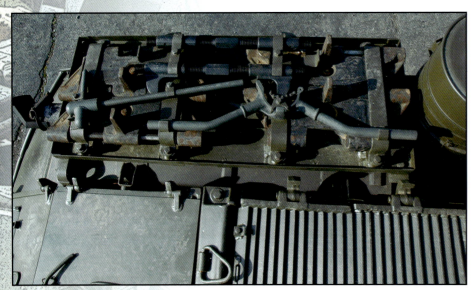

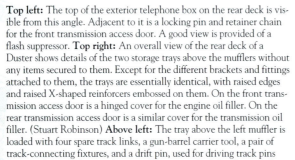

Top left: The top of the exterior telephone box on the rear deck is visible from this angle. Adjacent to it is a locking pin and retainer chain for the front transmission access door. A good view is provided of a flash suppressor. **Top right:** An overall view of the rear deck of a Duster shows details of the two storage trays above the mufflers without any items secured to them. Except for the different brackets and fittings attached to them, the trays are essentially identical, with raised edges and raised X-shaped reinforcers embossed on them. On the front transmission access door is a hinged cover for the engine oil filler. On the rear transmission access door is a similar cover for the transmission oil filler. (Stuart Robinson) **Above left:** The tray above the left muffler is loaded with four spare track links, a gun-barrel carrier tool, a pair of track-connecting fixtures, and a drift pin, used for driving track pins from track assemblies. To the rear of the tray is the left exhaust deflector. Note how the hinges of the engine grilles include stops to hold the grilles at a fixed angle when open. **Above right:** In an overhead view of the front left corner of the rear deck of a Duster, at the center is the hinged, armored cover for the fuel filler. There was only one fuel filler on the

Duster. Next to the fuel filler cover is the air filter inlet duct over the air outlet duct. The air-filter ducts are not symmetrically arranged: the inlet ducts are identifiable by their boxy, welded designs, while the outlets are round tubes. Also in view is the cover for the left rear 40mm ammunition compartment.